It Happened In Nebraska

Remarkable Events That Shaped History

D1738464

Tammy Partsch

Guilford, Connecticut

Map: Melissa Baker © 2012 by Rowman & Littlefield

Distributed by NATIONAL BOOK NETWORK

Library of Congress Cataloging-in-Publication Data on file.

ISBN: 978-0-7627-6971-1

Printed in the United States of America

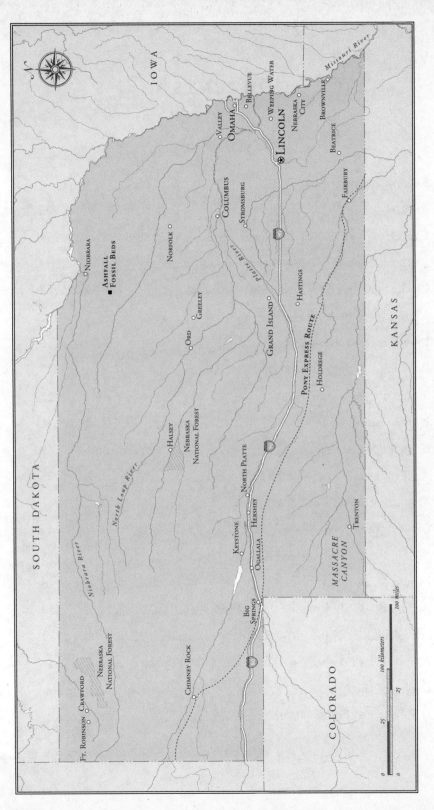

NEBRASKA

CONTENTS

CONTENTS

ACKNOWLEDGMENTS

Sincere thanks and acknowledgments . . .

. . . to Erin Turner and the editors at Globe Pequot Press for making this, and me, look good.

. . . to Rebecca Turner for directing me on this path.

. . . to Melissa Turner, great friend, and Chloe Higgins, future author, for ideas and encouragement.

. . . to Dean and Keitha Thomson for driving us all over the state as kids, showing us how beautiful Nebraska really is.

. . . to Luke Partsch for telling me to wake up and start writing. Here it is in print: I love you more.

. . . to David Partsch for your support and love and patience. Thanks for growing old with me. I love you.

PREFACE

When I first sat down to write this book, I thought it would be fairly easy; I figured I knew enough about Nebraska to make research a breeze. I was familiar with the stories and tales that made headlines. However, I was truly surprised about how much I didn't know about what I knew.

Let me explain that better. I knew Kool-Aid was invented in Nebraska, but I didn't know Edwin Perkins. Visiting the Hastings Museum of Natural & Cultural History taught me more about Perkins and his invention than I could ever hope to use in a chapter here, and it was all fascinating. I also knew that there was something called a canteen in North Platte and it did something for soldiers during World War II. Reading James Reisdorff's *North Platte Canteen* gave me the whole story and put into perspective what a huge and encompassing project it was.

There were some stories floating around about Nebraska that were obvious choices to include in a history on the state, like Kool-Aid and the North Platte Canteen. Standing Bear's trial and Daniel Freeman's inaugural Homestead claim were also easy choices.

But there were some stories that were more difficult to pin down; the tale of the steam wagon gives us an interesting glimpse into the past, but is a nonevent. In addition, while the invention of center pivot irrigation certainly equaled progress, there is continued conflict regarding use and possible pollution of the Ogallala Aquifer.

There were stories that made me teary: Massacre Canyon; Schoolchildren's Blizzard; Grand Island Tornadoes. There were stories that gave me hope: A Gift for the Future; He Ain't Heavy, He's M' Brother; Proving His Loyalty. I have been introduced to Nebraskans from various times in history in researching this book and have come away humbled by their ideals and work ethic.

It takes someone special to settle in a land commonly thought of as a desert. The people who made this state what it is today came from diverse cultural and socio-economic backgrounds. That melding together of morals and ingenuity helps make this state thrive. We have Czech, Polish, and German festivals; Hispanic celebrations; and Irish parties. We created Valentino's pizza, Runzas, and Dorothy Lynch Salad Dressing. We work hard in Nebraska, but we also play hard. We are the home of comedians Johnny Carson, Dick Cavett, and Larry the Cable Guy. Gerald Ford, Malcolm X, and Marlon Brando all called Omaha their birthplace. We support our native sons and daughters as they make their own way in this world and welcome them home with open arms.

I started writing this book when there was three feet of snow on the ground outside my window. I completed most of my research as the daffodils bloomed and the apple trees were budding. I wrote deep into the twilight nights of summer, listening to crickets in my garden. I made changes and corrections as russet and golden leaves fell around me and Husker football blared from my radio. In the year it took me to write this book, I have grown to love Nebraska more and more, for the people, the history, the geography, and the seasons.

It has truly been a blessing for me to write this book. I have lived in Nebraska nearly my entire life and have driven lengthwise across it more times than I can remember. This is my home, but I was blissfully unaware of how unique Nebraska really is. People from other states may read this and think, "Well, my state is pretty unique, too." And they will be right. What makes our home states extraordinary to us are the memories we have. Sometimes we can't appreciate those memories until we leave for a time. Sometimes it takes an event, like witnessing the outpouring of support after a tornado, to open our eyes. Sometimes it takes work, like months of research, before we can finally see how special home really is.

But for me, I truly believe there is no place like Nebraska.

GRAVEYARD WATERING HOLE

Twelve Million Years Ago

The ash fell like snow from the darkened sky. Several inches covered the ground and more was falling. By the time the ash stopped raining down onto the earth, over a foot had fallen on the savannah. The winds picked up and cleared ash from higher grounds, drifting it deep over the low-lying areas like snow falling on a barren prairie. The animals gathered at a watering hole did not understand the danger until it was too late.

The gently rolling farmland we see in northeast Nebraska now does not look like the prairie of twelve million years ago. During the age of the dinosaurs, Nebraska lay under a vast inland sea. As the eons rolled by, the seas receded. The dinosaurs disappeared and other animals began to evolve. Those animals closely resembled modern creatures, but there were differences. Three-toed horses, a giraffe-camel, four-tusked elephants; these were the creatures that wandered the warm, jungle-like plains twelve million years ago.

The ash fall was the result of a volcanic explosion that occurred a thousand miles away in what is now Idaho. The blast from the supervolcano has been classified as larger than both the Krakatoa explosion in 1883 and the Mount St. Helens explosion of 1980. Within hours, the ash spread like a blizzard to the east of the original explosion site, covering everything in its tracks.

The smaller creatures at the watering hole in northeast Nebraska were the first to die, just hours after the ash fall began: frogs, pond turtles, hedgehogs, birds. Over the next few days, medium-sized animals met their deaths as well, many from suffocation from the heavy ash fall. As horses, saber-toothed deer, and bone-crushing dogs, so named by scientists because of their powerful build, ate the ash-covered grass in the area, their lungs filled with ashy residue and their breathing became labored. The largest animals held on to life for a few weeks, but soon succumbed as well. These animals included barrel-bodied rhinos, camels, and even elephants.

The deaths were quick. The animals lay where they collapsed, often herded together. As the bodies piled up, so did the ash. The wind continued to blow, covering the carcasses with even more ash—up to ten feet deep. The ash protected the dead animal bodies from natural decay and also from scavengers.

Fast forward twelve million years.

It's a clear spring day in 1971. Heavy rains the day before had eroded part of a gully on the perimeter of a field belonging to a farmer named Melvin Colson. The dirty, gray skull of a baby rhino was exposed. Colson, intrigued by what he saw, immediately contacted the staff of the University of Nebraska State Museum. Museum paleontologists rushed to the site to investigate. As they carefully dug around the rhino skull, the complete skeleton soon emerged, with even the most delicate bones intact. Scientists were excited about the discovery; the ash preserved the skeletons in near-perfect condition, creating a snapshot of animal life during that time.

Ashfall Fossil Beds State Historical Park is now a designated National Natural Landmark. Excavation has been ongoing since the 1970s and more species are being uncovered each year. More than one hundred complete rhino skeletons have been uncovered, including a mother rhino with a fetus still intact in her belly. There have been more rhino skeletons than any other animal uncovered at the site.

In addition, more than fifty species of animals and plants have been identified at the site. There are familiar animals like shrews, moles, lizards, gophers, and bats. The unfamiliar species include the giraffe camel, a horned rodent, and an oreodont, which is a leaf-eating mammal.

Today, an eighteen-thousand-square-foot open air barn covers the current excavation site. Visitors can watch paleontologists at work in the barn, slowly and carefully brushing ash from skeletal remains. The Ashfall Fossil Beds site offers a glimpse into life in the area twelve million years ago.

BATTLE OF THE MAMMOTHS

Ten Thousand Years Ago

It was mating season. Two bull mammoths both had their eyes on one superb specimen of a female mammoth. She flirted with both and ignored both in equal amounts and their frustrations rose. It seemed imperative that one of them mate with her soon. The bull mammoths knew about each other. The huge animals had warily shared space, but now it was time to mate. There could be no more competition.

The mammoths might have been able to sense that big change was coming. Their time of roaming the vast plains of what is now North America was coming to a close. The Earth was warming and the Ice Age was ending.

One of the bull mammoths shook his shaggy head and bellowed a challenge to the other. His massive thirteen-foot frame rocked back and forth on tree trunk–sized legs as he dared his foe to come closer.

The other mammoth responded in kind. He lumbered up to the challenger and roared back, swinging his curved tusks back and forth.

The female mammoth watched with interest from a nearby hill. She would mate with the mammoth who won the fight, whichever proved to be the stronger animal.

The two bull mammoths met in a clash of ivory and fur, each trying to get the best of the other. Tusks slashed. Legs kicked. Heads butted.

The mammoths were evenly matched. The fight lasted most of the daylight hours. Finally, one of the mammoths twisted his head close to the other and locked their tusks together. Pushing and straining, he attempted to bring down his enemy.

The other mammoth struggled to get his tusks loose. He bellowed in fury and fear when he realized he was stuck. He couldn't break free.

The first mammoth knew he had won. He gathered up all his remaining strength and pushed one last time.

The second mammoth took a short step backward, but missed his footing and slipped. He went down hard and felt a searing pain in his head. The tusk from his opponent had gone right into his eye.

The beaten mammoth tried to rise, but he couldn't get his legs under himself. The pain from his wounds began to overwhelm him and he sank back on the ground. He knew he had lost.

The first mammoth bawled in victory and attempted to raise his head to look for his prize. But something was wrong. His head wouldn't move. He tugged harder and harder to no avail. The tusks of the winner and loser were so tightly twisted together that the winner could not get loose.

The mammoth tried all through the night to get free. The other mammoth lay where he had died, his body weight prohibiting the winning mammoth from untangling the tusks.

Finally, the mammoth gave up. Rolling his eyes toward where the female had been during the fight, he saw her turn and walk away. She would mate with neither one now. They had both failed.

The days passed and the mammoth grew weaker. He continued to try, in vain, to free himself from his prison. Finally, his knees buckled and he sank to the ground in front of his foe. His time was over as well.

Ten thousand years later, long after the Ice Age passed and humans populated the area, the remains of the woolly mammoths were found. In July of 1962, an electrical line was being laid on a ranch near Crawford, Nebraska. Two soil conservation workers spotted a large bone poking out of the earth. They halted their work and took the bone to local University of Nebraska State Museum employees. Digging soon began in the area and the body of a mammoth was uncovered.

The workers were surprised to find a large tusk positioned with its point coming toward the mammoth and at first assumed the tusk had broken off the animal when it died. Soon, however, more digging showed the intertwined tusks and the second mammoth. Just as the mammoths couldn't get free of each other ten thousand years ago, neither could the museum workers untangle the tusks. The bodies of the mammoths were removed from the ground in one large piece with the tusks still joined.

How the two animals died is not known for certain, although the story illustrated above is the accepted theory. Soon after the mammals died, their bodies were covered with a thick layer of silt and preserved in excellent condition. The remains are now displayed at the Trailside Museum of Natural History in Fort Robinson State Park, just a few miles from where they were found and where they had lain for thousands of years.

PRIVATE SHANNON GETS LOST

1804

Private George Shannon knew that today was the day he was destined to die. His body was weak from lack of food. Fresh water was in short supply. He was out of ammunition for his gun.

Shannon stood on the south bank of the Missouri River. It was September 11, 1804, and he had been wandering in what is now northeast Nebraska for nearly two weeks, living on wild grapes and a rabbit he had killed by shooting a sharpened stick from the barrel of his gun.

But the food was gone and so was Shannon's energy. He sank to his knees on the muddy bank and then leaned back against a tree. He would wait here for a trading boat. They sometimes came south on the Missouri River from the Mandan Indian villages in the Dakotas to the north. Sometimes. Shannon rubbed his tired eyes. He didn't really want to die; he was only twenty years old, the youngest member of the Corps of Discovery under the command of Meriwether Lewis and William Clark. Only he wasn't part of the Corps any more. They were long gone, Shannon was sure, on their way west to find passage to the Pacific Ocean. Shannon had been so proud to have been chosen to join the Corps.

Private George Shannon knew the chances of a trading boat finding him in time were slim. He closed his eyes and fell asleep, all alone, on the banks of the Missouri River.

<center>~~~</center>

Two weeks earlier, on August 27, 1804, Private Shannon had volunteered to search for a herd of horses that had gotten separated from the main group. He never returned. To the men of the Corps, the disappearance of Shannon was a distressing blow.

Meriwether Lewis and William Clark, the leaders of the Corps of Discovery, had little hope they would ever find Private Shannon. The two men stood at the prow of the keelboat that was being rowed upstream by a determined group of men. Shannon was the second loss for the Corps; Sergeant Charles Floyd had died just a few weeks prior from a mystery illness (probably acute appendicitis). Lewis and Clark were discussing what, if anything, could be done to help find Shannon.

"I don't want to send any more of our men out to look for him," Clark said to Lewis in a low tone. "Private Colter went searching for Shannon and the lost horses but didn't find a trace of either one."

Lewis nodded in agreement. "President Jefferson wants our mission to succeed," he said, "even if that means we lose a few men. I don't think there is anything more we can do for Shannon."

Lewis gazed back at the men struggling to move the keelboat farther upriver. The Corps was a group of about three dozen men, all picked by Lewis for this arduous journey west. The Corps had begun their adventure in May of 1804 and had no idea how long it would take to cross the uncharted land of middle America. All of the men knew there were unknown dangers awaiting them on their journey, but so far, with the exception of the death of Sergeant Floyd, things had gone fairly smoothly.

This was all President Thomas Jefferson's idea. The year before, in 1803, Jefferson had negotiated with France to purchase the Louisiana Territory. The land, which measured nearly 830,000 square miles, had never been fully explored by France and now it belonged to the United States. The Louisiana Territory stretched from the Gulf of Mexico in the South to the Rocky Mountains in the West. With the purchase of the territory, the United States doubled her size.

Jefferson asked Meriwether Lewis, his personal secretary, to lead a group of men across the wilderness and find a water route to the West Coast. Lewis, William Clark, and more than thirty others signed up for the mission. They were concerned about disease and sickness, such as what had killed Sergeant Floyd, but their biggest worries were of the Indians they knew were out there.

Lewis suddenly straightened and pointed ahead to a low spot on the south bank of the river. "Look there," he shouted. "Is that a man?"

The keelboat surged to the left as the men tried to bring her in close to the bank. There, under the shade of a cottonwood tree, was Private George Shannon.

—◆—

". . . A man had like to have Starved to death in a land of Plenty for the want of Bulletes or Something to kill his meat."

Meriwether Lewis closed his journal and looked at the man sleeping on the pallet beside him. Private Shannon had been near death when they found him under the cottonwood tree. Lewis still had trouble believing Shannon was alive. Shannon had spoken a little of his two weeks alone in the wilderness, and swore that if he ever was away from the Corps again he would take extra bullets for his gun. Shannon had also said he firmly believed the Corps had already traveled ahead of him on the Missouri River, steadily working their way westward. He didn't know how many miles he had covered since he left the Corps in late August to search for the lost horses, but he always stayed to the south of the Missouri River.

After nursing Shannon back to health, the Corps moved onward and westward, searching for a waterway that would take them straight to the Pacific Ocean. Although they never did find such a waterway, the mission was deemed a success when the Corps returned east two years later. Sergeant Floyd was the only fatality. The Indians met by the Corps on their journey were friendly and helpful, for the most part, and even helped the Corps by providing food and guides.

Meriwether Lewis continued to record tidbits in his journal, including new and unusual plants and animals encountered by the Corps. He also wrote again of Private Shannon, this time from what is now Montana, where Shannon managed to get lost again. This time, Shannon found his way back to the Corps in only three days and used his fully loaded gun to kill several deer for food.

After the mission was completed, it didn't take long for others to explore the new land. Within fifty years, thousands of settlers and pioneers worked their way across the territory to the West Coast, many stopping along the way to build new homes and towns. Eventually the 830,000 square miles of the Louisiana Purchase was divided into fifteen US states and two Canadian provinces.

As for Private George Shannon, he returned successfully from his traveling adventure and studied law. Shannon settled in Missouri and worked as an attorney and also a senator. Although he did well in his life, Shannon is usually only remembered for getting lost.

CHIMNEY ON THE PLAINS

1855

The wagon rocked back and forth uncomfortably as it rolled across the prairie. Well, it would have been uncomfortable if Ellie hadn't been used to it. For the past month, Ellie and her family had been traveling on the famed Oregon Trail through Nebraska. At first, when her father had brought up traveling west to seek their fortune, Ellie had been thrilled. The trip would be such an adventure! Indians, flash floods, tornadoes . . . Ellie was excited to witness these events.

However, so far at least, the trip had been dull and long. The wagons were bulky and cumbersome and could only make fifteen miles a day, twenty if they were lucky. There were only twenty-one wagons in their group and Ellie was the only child. She didn't have anyone to talk to and was getting tired of talking to the oxen pulling the wagon. They never responded and they smelled bad. The most exciting part of the trip had been their stop at the military outpost, Fort Kearny, a couple of weeks ago. Even though the outpost was in the middle of nowhere, it allowed Ellie a change from the endless swaying of the wagon and she had spied her very first Indian. But now they were back on the trail and there wasn't an Indian in sight.

Ellie and her family were headed to California. Since gold was discovered there six years ago, thousands of fortune-hunters from the East had taken this very same trail west to be a part of the Gold Rush. Ellie's dad thought there was enough gold for everyone, but Ellie's mom was more concerned about their future. She had an idea of opening a general store wherever they decided to settle.

Ellie knew that fortune-hunters in the Gold Rush weren't the only ones to take this trail west, although they made up about half. Her dad told her about the settlers heading to Oregon and the Mormons who went as far as Utah Territory. She knew the trip would take about four months from start to finish.

Ellie also knew the trip wasn't without danger. Already, they had passed countless graves of those poor souls who died along the way. There weren't any proper cemeteries established yet and the dead were buried in the hard sod along the side of the trail. Some had makeshift gravestones carved from limestone rocks scattered around the prairie, but the farther west they traveled, limestone was harder and harder to find. Ellie spotted a dark shape on the horizon and sat up quickly. Then she slouched down again when she recognized the shape as that of a soddy. Those strange houses were actually made out of dirt! Ellie's dad had explained this to Ellie, too. Some of the pioneers had despaired of ever reaching California or Oregon and gave up to settle on the plains. There were hardly any trees on the prairie, so those settlers plowed up sections of dirt and grass roots, piled the sections on top of one another, and called the whole thing a house. Ellie was appalled! These people were actually living in dirt! Ellie's dad said soddies were actually a good idea as the dirt kept the homes cool in the summer and warm in the winter, but Ellie still disliked the whole idea.

Still, the soddies were better than the dugouts often spotted along stream banks. The dugouts were just as the name implied: homes dug out of the earth! They didn't have any windows and the fronts were covered with blankets or buffalo hides to keep out the wind and bad weather.

Ellie wanted to live in a log cabin like the one they had lived in before they left Illinois. Her dad said there were many trees in California and they wouldn't have any trouble finding wood to build their new house, but Ellie had her doubts after seeing the way these settlers lived in Nebraska.

As the wagon train continued across the prairie, Ellie thought of how strange the whole process was. Their wagon train wasn't really a train at all; instead of going in a single line on the trail, the train was spread out at least a mile wide, the oxen and wagon wheels stirring up dust and dirt. Ellie took to wearing a handkerchief tied across her mouth and nose to keep out the dust and, at her mother's insistence, wore an old bonnet on her head to protect her from the sun. She thought she looked ridiculous.

What was also ridiculous was the amount of stuff that was left on the side of the trail. In just a three-mile stretch yesterday, Ellie had spotted a trunk full of dishes, two chairs, and a piano. A piano! Ellie asked her dad why anyone would want to bring an old piano to California anyway. Ellie's dad said some people packed everything they had and brought it all. Ellie then asked why they ended up throwing it away on the side of the trail. Ellie's dad said that the heavier the wagon was the slower it would go and some people found that out the hard way. Ellie's dad said all the stuff on the side of the trail was deemed too heavy to keep as the trail went on.

So far, Ellie's family hadn't needed to throw out any of their possessions. Their only casualty was Ellie's porcelain doll that she brought from home. It had dropped off the wagon and had been crushed under the wagon's heavy wheels. Ellie had been heartbroken until her mother had stitched together what she called a "Wagon Train Doll" from old pieces of cloth and quilts. Ellie liked her new doll almost as much as the old one and this one wouldn't break.

The wagon wheels slipped out of their ruts and the wagon jerked heavily to the side. The sudden movement tossed Ellie off the back of the wagon seat into the wagon itself. Luckily, she landed on a pile of blankets her mother had just washed in the nearby Platte River. The wagons moved so slowly that it was pretty easy for Ellie's mother to walk to the river and back with a bucket of water and do the wash while the train was in motion. She had asked Ellie to help a couple of times, but because Ellie kept dropping the heavy buckets of water, her mother gave up and let her just ride on the wagon seat with her dad.

Ellie climbed back onto the seat and smiled up at her dad. He grinned back and pointed ahead of their wagon. "Look, Ellie," he said. "We're coming up on Chimney Rock."

Ellie squinted into the setting sun. She could barely make out a slender spire rising up from the plains. "What's Chimney Rock, Dad?" she asked.

Ellie's dad flicked the reins he was holding. "Well, the soldiers at Fort Kearny said it's a tall tower made of clay."

"Clay?" Ellie asked.

"Yup, a special kind of clay found in this part of Nebraska," her dad said. "They think the clay is layered with volcanic ash, even though there aren't any volcanoes in the area. The column is about five hundred feet tall."

"That's really tall," said Ellie. After weeks of flat grasslands, she couldn't imagine anything that tall. "Are there other mountains around it?" she asked.

"It's not exactly a mountain, sweetie," her dad said. "It's more of a rock formation. And, yes, there are other formations nearby, including Jail Rock and Courthouse Rock."

Ellie laughed. "Those are funny names!" she said.

"Yes, they probably are," said her dad. "But those names describe how they look pretty well. Like Chimney Rock. See how it's wide at the bottom and narrows to a point at the top, like a chimney?"

Ellie looked ahead. They were closer to Chimney Rock now and she could make out more details. It really did look like a chimney! As the wagon train approached the natural structure, the men of the train decided to stop for the night in its shadow.

They circled the wagons in their usual protective formation and started a cooking fire. Ellie climbed the base of Chimney Rock and stared up at its top. The setting sun bathed the spire in a golden light. Ellie turned and saw her dad approaching carrying a large knife.

"What are you doing, Dad?" Ellie asked as she climbed down.

"We're going to be a part of history, Ellie," her dad replied. He took his knife and carefully carved their family name and the date in the soft clay of Chimney Rock. Ellie looked around and noticed other names and dates from past wagon trains. The entire base of Chimney Rock seemed covered in lettering.

Ellie's dad stood and held his arms out to Ellie. She hugged him tightly.

"Are we really a part of history, Dad?" she asked.

"We sure are," he answered.

"Wow," she said. "That is really the adventure I was hoping for!"

JOHN BROWN'S CAVE

1859

Barbara Kagi Mayhew gripped the top of the ladder with both hands and peered into the dark gloom of the loft. All was quiet. The boys were sleeping soundly, their chests rising and falling with regularity. It was bitterly cold this February night and the Mayhew family had prepared for the chill by bringing in extra horse blankets from the barn. Those blankets now covered Barbara's sons as they slept.

Barbara lowered herself down the ladder and into the main room of the cabin. Her husband, Allen, looked up from where he was whittling by the woodstove.

"Are they asleep?" he asked his wife.

Barbara nodded and slipped into her rocking chair next to Allen. "Any sign of John?" she asked.

Allen shook his head and got up to peer out the window. The glass window was a luxury for this family near the small town of Nebraska City on the Missouri River; the cabin only had two windows for the entire structure. The Mayhews weren't rich by any means, but they were comfortable.

Barbara picked up her needle and thread and began to repair a hole in the toe of her last good pair of thick, wool stockings. All this waiting was making her nervous. Her brother, John, had sent word he would arrive sometime tonight with a special cargo. She knew that meant he was traveling with escaped slaves from somewhere in the South, perhaps even as close as Missouri. His letter had arrived a few days ago from Kansas, so Barbara knew John was on the move.

What concerned Barbara the most was that she feared her brother John was traveling with the famed abolitionist John Brown. Not that Barbara was afraid of John Brown; she supported his anti-slavery stance and actions. But Brown was a wanted man, and that put their whole group in danger. For all Barbara knew, her own brother could be a wanted man, too! And he was leading the "cargo" right to her house, where her small, innocent boys slept.

Barbara wasn't naïve. She knew what had been happening in Kansas these past few years since the United States Congress passed the Kansas-Nebraska Act. The act, which passed in 1854, organized a large chunk of the Louisiana Purchase into two territories, Kansas and Nebraska. The idea of creating states in the plains originated in the need for a safe route for a transcontinental railroad, which was still just a dream. But the idea turned into something more when the act's main supporter, Senator Stephen A. Douglas, a Democrat from Illinois, included the plan to repeal the 1820 Missouri Compromise. The compromise decreed that each new state to enter the union would enter as a free state, not a slave state. Douglas, in order to get the bill passed, rejected the Missouri Compromise and introduced "popular sovereignty," which gave each new state the choice of whether to be a free state or slave state.

The act passed, but brought with it violence and unrest. The term "Bleeding Kansas" was coined to refer to how much blood was spilled between anti-slavery and pro-slavery groups in Kansas and Missouri over the past five years. Nebraska, where the Mayhews lived, had been spared most of the violence, but it was not immune. While most new settlers to Nebraska did not own slaves, there were a few who did, including the man credited with founding Nebraska City, Stephen F. Nuckolls. Just a year ago, in 1858, two of Nuckolls's five slaves escaped from his home in Nebraska City. With help from local abolitionists, they crossed the Missouri River and fled into Iowa. Nuckolls had followed the female slaves all the way to Chicago, but returned home empty-handed.

A knock at the door startled Barbara. Allen quickly moved to the door and yelled, "Who's there?"

"Allen? Barbara? It's me, your brother John," came the reply.

Allen eased open the door and a lanky form slipped in. John Kagi was a tall man, nearing six feet, but he was slim. To Barbara's eyes, he seemed just skin and bones. She knew he refused to eat meat and her mothering instinct arose in her. She had raised John and their sister Mary since their mother died young and now viewed him more as a son than a brother.

"John," she breathed, rushing to him and embracing him strongly. "Are you safe?"

John Kagi looked down at his sister and smiled. "I'm fine, Barbara, thank you."

Allen looked out into the darkness one more time before closing the door. "Are you alone, John?"

John turned to Allen and looked between him and Barbara. "I am, at the moment," he replied. "I am not traveling alone, but I have taken pains to hide my cargo."

Barbara pulled John over to the woodstove and offered him a chair. John sat and warmed his hands by the fire. Little by little, he told the Mayhews of his doings the past few years.

As Barbara feared, it was a story fraught with danger. John Kagi had been fired from his job as a schoolteacher in Virginia after making anti-slavery comments in public. He soon became involved in the Underground Railroad, the name given to a series of routes that escaped slaves took from the South to free lands in the North. He spent some time in prison for his anti-slavery sentiment, although he was never tried. He even was wounded in a shooting match with a judge in Kansas!

But the biggest news brother John had was his interaction with Kansas abolitionist John Brown. Brown and John Kagi had traveled together all over the country and even into Canada to spread word of their anti-slavery stance. Now John was on the run again, this time from authorities in Kansas over the killing of a deputy marshal.

John looked at Barbara. "I know you must be worried about your boys, Barbara," he said, "so I left the men in your old dugout for the night."

Barbara frowned. The old dugout was on the edge of their property, near the creek. Barbara and Allen had lived in the natural cave when they first arrived in Nebraska City years ago and now used it to store wine and food.

"Is it warm enough?" she asked her brother.

John smiled. "Well, there are more than a dozen of us, including Mr. Brown, and we are packed in there pretty tight, so we should be okay."

Barbara inhaled sharply. John Brown was with them! If the authorities found out, they would be ruthless in hunting down all members of the party and perhaps even those who had helped them along the way.

John Kagi smiled at his sister. "Barbara, I know you are concerned, but we are on the edge of something greater than ourselves. Mr. Brown has an idea to help the slaves in the South, and the time is almost here!"

John went on to outline Brown's plan. Sometime the following summer or fall, Brown and a small band of followers, including Kagi, would sneak into an arsenal in a small town in West Virginia by the name of Harpers Ferry. Brown was planning on stealing the arsenal's weapons and distributing them to slaves throughout the South. He would then lead them in a revolt against slave owners.

Barbara knew her brother was passionate about abolishing slavery. However, a feeling of dread stole over her as she listened to the plan. She didn't think any good would come out of it, but she knew nothing she could say would make a difference to her brother.

After talking late into the night, Barbara and Allen offered their pallet in the loft to John for the night, but he refused, saying he wanted to stay with his men. Promising to return for breakfast, John left the cabin and headed into the dark night.

The next morning dawned clear and cold. Even before the sun cleared the bluffs to the east, John Kagi led his "cargo" of escaped slaves from the cave to the front door of the Mayhew cabin.

Barbara counted fourteen black men, of all shapes and sizes, in the yard behind her brother John. John Brown was nowhere to be found.

"He went on ahead," John Kagi said, knowing what his sister was thinking.

Allen invited the men into the cabin and Barbara began serving a quick breakfast of biscuits and oatmeal. No one spoke much until Edward, the Mayhew's oldest son, glanced out the window and shouted in alarm.

Barbara rushed to the window and, with a sinking heart, saw the area's deputy marshal astride a horse in the front yard, a rifle slung across his saddle. Behind him were a few men from town, men whom Barbara knew to be pro-slavery. A slight noise behind Barbara made her whirl around in time to see a pair of legs disappear up the ladder into the sleeping loft. Allen looked up into the loft, nodded at something, and turned toward the door.

"What are you going to do?" Barbara hissed at him.

"Buy them some time," The main room was now empty. Allen replied and opened the front door.

The deputy marshal was a big man with a big voice. He hailed Allen and then said, "I know John Kagi is here with slaves, Allen Mayhew. I am here to arrest him."

Allen nodded slowly. "He is, Deputy Marshal. I won't deny it. I will tell you, though, that he is armed and is a very good shot."

Several of the men behind the deputy marshal stirred and muttered to themselves.

Allen continued, "Please let me and my wife leave this property with our children. They are young, and I want to keep them safe."

The deputy marshal considered these words and finally agreed. He rose in his stirrups and spoke to his men. "I know John Kagi is a killer and an excellent shot. We will need reinforcements." He looked again at Allen. "We will be back," he said and wheeled his horse around, riding hard back to town, his small posse following.

Almost before they were out of sight, there was movement at the front door of the cabin. John Kagi, followed by fourteen black men, slipped out the door. While the escaped slaves darted for the woods behind the house, John came up to Barbara.

"I'm sorry to have put your family in danger," he said as he hugged her hard. "We'll lose them in the woods by the river."

"Good luck," Barbara responded. She watched as John disappeared into the woods, wondering if she would ever see him again.

John Kagi was killed in John Brown's doomed raid on Harpers Ferry, West Virginia, in October 1859. The raid is considered by some to have been the starting point of the Civil War, which officially ended slavery in America. Barbara Kagi Mayhew's husband, Allen, died in 1862. Barbara married abolitionist Calvin B. Bradway in 1865; he was murdered, perhaps for his anti-slavery ideas, in 1869. Barbara continued to live in the Nebraska City area until her death in 1882.

Slavery never did become the norm in Nebraska City; the year after John Kagi visited his sister at her cabin with his "cargo," Stephen Nuckolls's remaining three slaves also escaped using the Underground Railroad. Also in 1860, six slaves belonging to Nebraska City freighting magnate Alexander Majors fled to freedom. Majors, one of the founders of the Russell, Majors, and Waddell Freighting Company, offered a one-thousand-dollar reward for the return of his slaves, but they were long gone.

The Mayhew Cabin, the home of Alexander Majors, and the site of Stephen Nuckolls's home are all officially recognized by the National Park Service as part of the National Underground Railroad Network. They are the only such listings in Nebraska.

PONY EXPRESS SUCCESS

1860

Communication between the East and West Coasts of America was different in the 1860s than it is today. There was no Internet, no e-mail, no telephones. Messages were sent using the US Postal Service, but that service was limited to the coasts. Letters and packages that went across the country had to travel by stagecoach through the southern part of the United States, a trip that often took weeks.

As the West Coast became more and more populated, the need for a fast, reliable transcontinental mail delivery service became evident. In the early spring of 1860, William H. Russell, a partner in the Nebraska City–based shipping company of Russell, Majors, and Waddell, was approached by a senator from California with the idea of establishing a direct route of communication across the Rocky Mountains. Russell, Majors, and Waddell were already running a daily stagecoach from the Missouri River to Salt Lake City, Utah. The idea was to create a continuous relay of fast horses along the same trail and extend it into California.

Russell had to talk fast to convince his partners Majors and Waddell to agree to the venture. Their initial cost was just under one hundred thousand dollars, which was used to purchase equipment and horses and to pay employees. Majors and Waddell did not think the idea was economically viable, but Russell changed their minds.

The project was soon named "The Pony Express." The fifteen-hundred-mile route was divided into segments, with 190 stations placed at regular intervals, every ten to twelve miles. Each station had a manager and a place for the riders to change horses. The stations were small and cramped, with little in the way of amenities. Station managers were responsible for the care of the horses, cleaning and feeding them in between rides.

The men hired by Russell, Majors, and Waddell to ride the Pony Express were a special breed. Advertisements appeared in major newspapers: "Wanted: Young, skinny, wiry fellows not over 18. Must be expert pony riders willing to risk death daily. Orphans preferred." Each rider took an oath not to drink, swear, or fight with other employees. They were outfitted with signature blue pants and red tops and each were given a Bible and a gun. The Pony Express employed up to eighty riders and owned five hundred horses.

The riders were responsible for fifty to one hundred miles per trip. Upon arrival at the next station along the route, riders would quickly dismount and stretch their legs while the station manager transferred the mail bags from the tired pony to a fresh one. After a quick bite to eat, the rider would mount his new pony and be on his way.

The messages carried by the Pony Express riders were written on tissue paper to keep the weight down. Each message cost five dollars. The messages were placed in special saddlebags designed to be easy to transfer from mount to mount.

The first Pony Express ride took off in April of 1860, with one rider leaving St. Joseph, Missouri, heading west, and another rider

leaving Sacramento, California, heading east. The westbound route
went from St. Joseph to Marysville, Kansas, crossed into Nebraska to
Fort Kearny, followed the Platte River Valley to Julesburg, Colorado,
cut across the panhandle of Nebraska to Fort Laramie, Wyoming,
then headed west to Salt Lake City, Utah, and Friday's Station,
Nevada, and ending in Sacramento, California. There were thirty-
seven stations in Nebraska, the most of any state.

The average delivery time was shortened from several weeks
by stagecoach to only ten days by Pony Express. The record for
east-west delivery was made in March of 1861, when riders carried
President Abraham Lincoln's inaugural address across the country in
seven days, seventeen hours.

There were many dangers along the Pony Express route, from
inclement weather to hostile Indians. There were internal dangers as
well. A manager hired by Russell, Majors, and Waddell to work the
Rock Creek, Nebraska, station, owed a local man some money. When
the man came to collect, the station manager shot him in cold blood.
The station manager was not jailed for murder, even though the other
man was unarmed at the time of the shooting. The station manager
was named James Butler Hickok. He later served as a spy in the Civil
War and as a marshal and scout for the US Army before traveling with
Buffalo Bill Cody's Wild West Show as Wild Bill Hickok.

During the entire run of the Pony Express, only one rider was
killed by Indians and only one scheduled run was not completed.
Perhaps even more astounding is the fact that only one piece of mail
was lost.

For all the romance associated with the Pony Express, it was
doomed almost from the start. The cost of sending a message on the
Pony Express was deemed too steep for a majority of individuals and
the only ones who used it with any regularity were government and
military organizations. It took longer for those entities to appropriate

funds for the project, so Russell, Majors, and Waddell often had to borrow money to pay their expenses. In the end, Russell, Majors, and Waddell went bankrupt because of how much they had invested in the Pony Express.

The Pony Express was also doomed by the advent of new technology. The telegraph had been in use in the East since the mid-1800s and the transcontinental telegraph, linking the East and West Coasts, was completed in October of 1861. The Pony Express officially ceased operations two days after the transcontinental telegraph was completed, after only eighteen months in business.

STEAM WAGON

1862

Sam pushed his way through to the front of the crowd gathered at the levee. The muddy Missouri River was running high that day, but the crowd was not interested in the river. They were focused on the steamboat churning its way up the river from the south. The steamboat, named *West Wind,* was carrying something new and exciting, although Sam did not really understand it all.

It was July 14, 1862, and excitement was running high in the river town of Nebraska City in the Nebraska Territory. For several months, the editor of the *Nebraska City News,* J. Sterling Morton, had written about a new venture coming to the community: a traction engine. The idea was to develop a direct shipping route between Nebraska City and Denver in the Colorado Territory by use of a steam-powered wagon.

Morton's interest in the steam wagon originated in his friendship with Joe Brown, a newspaper editor from Minnesota. Brown also was a businessman and trader and even worked as an Indian agent for the United States. Brown, Morton, and Alexander Majors of Russell, Majors, and Waddell Freighting Company had worked together to bring this new machine to Nebraska City.

Traction engines had been in use for over a decade in industrialized nations. Replacing horses and oxen, the engines were powered by steam and eliminated the need for caring for live animals. And, unlike trains, the traction engines did not depend on tracks to go where they needed.

Sam and the rest of the Nebraska City crowd did not care too much about the history of traction engines. They were more interested in seeing if this product would benefit their community. Nebraska City was already a jumping off point for many settlers traveling west, but there was talk about a new railroad coming to the territory. If the government chose another city to host the railroad, Nebraska City's prominence would be lost.

As Sam watched in fascination from his spot at the front of the crowd, townsmen wrestled a large, tarp-covered machine off the steamboat and onto the dock. A fierce-looking gentleman with dark hair stepped to the side and raised his arms to quite the crowd. He looked out over the expectant faces and began to speak.

"Ladies and gentlemen of Nebraska City, thank you for your interest in our little adventure," he said. "I am Joe Brown and this is the *Prairie Motor!*"

With a flourish, Brown untied the tarp and flung it away from the machine underneath. The crowd gasped to see such a contraption! Large metal wheels supported the heavy frame, and hoses and wires and tubes led every which way around the machine. Brown fiddled a bit with the controls and the machine roared to life. Sam was in awe. He had never heard such noise!

Brown stepped down from the dock and was greeted by J. Sterling Morton, the editor. The two men shook hands. Brown directed his workmen to steer the *Prairie Motor* through town to the Morton farm to the west.

For the next several days, the *Prairie Motor* could be seen around town, taking people for rides and hooking up wagons to test the strength of the motor. Brown made himself available to the people of Nebraska City during that time. He patiently answered questions about how the *Prairie Motor* worked. Even though Brown wasn't an engineer by trade, he had designed the machine and knew its inner workings. Sam, who was friends with J. Sterling Morton's sons, rode the *Prairie Motor* several times a day.

At five o'clock on the evening of July 22, 1862, one week and one day after the *Prairie Motor* arrived in Nebraska City, it began its inaugural journey, towing three large wagons full of freight. The steam wagon also carried two cords of wood, or 256 cubic feet. As Brown had indicated, the final destination of the *Prairie Motor* was Denver.

Workmen fired up the *Prairie Motor* and turned it west. The crowd at the Morton farm cheered as the wagon pulled away. Brown waved to the crowd from his spot on the wagon, a smile creasing his face.

That smile did not last long. Just under three miles into the journey, the *Prairie Motor* suddenly jerked to a stop. Brown and his workmen climbed down from the wagon and inspected the motor. A part in the engine had broken, but that wasn't the worst news. Brown frowned as his engineers told him the news: They didn't have a replacement part and no one else in the Nebraska Territory did, either. They would have to go back to New York to get what they needed.

The workmen pushed the broken wagon off to the side of the road and headed back to town. A few days later, they returned and pushed the wagon to the Morton farm to wait for repairs.

Brown was disappointed and left Nebraska City for New York to get the new part. Three of his engineers stayed and waited for Brown to return. After a few months, with no word from Brown, two of the engineers left to seek other employment. The third engineer made Nebraska City his home.

The *Prairie Motor* stayed at the Morton farm. Sam and his friends would climb on the wagon and pretend to be engineers. Men from town came to look at the wagon and salvaged the iron for other community projects. One of the wheels even became a flowerbed.

The years passed. The county voters approved a special twenty-five-hundred-dollar bond to improve the road and build bridges, but the work was for nothing. One year after the *Prairie Motor* made her debut, Omaha was designated as the terminus for the new railroad and the climate of overland freight hauling changed once again.

Joe Brown never did return to Nebraska City. He left New York City to return home to Minnesota to help tamp down Indian uprisings. He died a few years later.

The road that marked the beginning of the steam wagon became known, naturally, as Steam Wagon Road. Today, on the county road about three miles west of Nebraska City, a stone monument marks the spot where the *Prairie Motor,* once a fine dream, died.

HOMESTEADING

1863

Daniel Freeman pounded on the door to the land office. It was just after midnight on January 1, 1863. Freeman, a Union soldier, had slipped up to Brownville, Nebraska, from his post at Fort Leavenworth, Kansas, with one thing on his mind. He wanted land.

Freeman raised his fist to knock on the door again when suddenly it opened from the inside. A man stood in the doorway holding a lantern in one hand. He peered out into the night at Freeman.

"Yes? Can I help you?" he said. Freeman's summons at the front door of the land office had clearly roused the man from sleep, as his hair was standing on end and his long nightgown was rumpled.

"I am sorry to have awakened you, sir," began Freeman, "but I am here to apply for my free land."

The land agent shook his head. "The Homestead Act does not become law until January 1. That's tomorrow." He moved to shut the door.

Freeman quickly wedged his boot in the door and held up his pocket watch.

"Sir, it *is* tomorrow."

The land agent squinted at the pocket watch then looked at Freeman again. "Well, if you are that anxious to have your land you can come on in, I guess." He backed up and opened the door fully.

Freeman nodded his thanks and followed the man into the land office. He could see an open door to the rear of the main room that obviously led to the land agent's private quarters. He caught sight of a corner of a rumpled blanket with a ceramic chamber pot peeking out from underneath the bed.

The land agent set his lantern down on a polished wooden desk in the middle of the main room. He muttered to himself as he sorted through scraps of papers.

"Aha! Here is it," said the man. He handed the sheet over to Freeman and passed him a quill.

By the soft light of the lantern, Freeman scanned through the document in his hands. For a twelve-dollar fee, he would receive 160 acres of fertile land of his choosing in the Nebraska Territory. This was the result of the Homestead Act Congress had passed the previous year, which President Abraham Lincoln had signed into law. The premise of the Homestead Act was to modernize the West and reduce poverty and overcrowding in the big cities of the East. Lincoln also wanted to establish more free states to help with his desire to end slavery in the United States.

Besides the small fee, the land was free to anyone over twenty-one, male or female, including freed slaves and immigrants. The only catch was the citizen had five years to cultivate the land and build a structure on it. At the end of that five-year period, the citizen would receive a title to the land free and clear.

Freeman had already picked out a site near a small Nebraska settlement called Beatrice, about sixty miles to the west of Brownville. The land he was interested in was near the freight road and a source of running water, Cub Creek. Freeman thought it would be just about perfect.

With a flourish of the quill, Freeman signed his claim. It was ten minutes after midnight on January 1, 1863. Freeman had just become the first person to apply for land under the nation's Homestead Act.

From that point on, more than 270 million acres were given away in thirty states over the next hundred-plus years. Although the Homestead Act was repealed in 1976, Alaska continued the program until the mid-1980s.

During its run, 10 percent of US land was distributed through the Homestead Act. However, only 40 percent of those who applied stayed on their land for the requisite five years. Of the other 60 percent, most gave up due to adverse conditions, such as blizzards, drought, grasshopper invasions, or simply the lack of knowledge to work the land.

The Homestead Act is often praised as being one of the first legislative actions that was equal to both men and women and to both whites and blacks. In fact, the Homestead Act became effective the same day as Lincoln's famed Emancipation Proclamation. However, the act did not provide for Native Americans; in fact, by 1900, 95 percent of American Indian land was lost to homesteading and other land action.

Even though Daniel Freeman applied for his claim in 1863, he had to wait two more years to move to Nebraska and start his new life. In 1865, Freeman finished his military service and started west to his new homestead in Nebraska. Along the way, he picked up his new bride, Agnes. Freeman and Agnes became engaged via a series of letters written between the two during the Civil War. Agnes had originally been engaged to Freeman's brother who was killed in action.

Freeman knew immediately he had made an excellent choice when he surveyed his property near Beatrice. Cub Creek ran full and fresh and the freight road from town was very close. Freeman got to work clearing the land of its native tall grasses and planted crops using an iron plow. He raised corn, wheat, and oats, along with growing a small orchard of apple and peach trees.

Even though Nebraska was mostly a treeless prairie, Freeman found there were a few trees growing on the banks of Cub Creek. He felled these trees for his log cabin and other wooden outbuildings and used the scraps of lumber as fuel.

One thing Freeman learned about life on the plains was how to make a fence when you didn't have fence materials. Freeman planted a row of Osage orange trees and trained the young shoots to grow horizontal to the ground. By doing so, Freeman could weave the branches together to form a living fence. The process took many years to complete, but, as Freeman found out, Osage orange was such a hard wood and made such a solid fence that it was worth it.

In addition to the crops tended by Freeman, he raised hogs, chickens, and horses. He also relied on his previous medical training and served as a physician for the citizens of Beatrice. Eventually the log cabin gave way to a two-story brick house. Freeman also built a school outside of Beatrice, which was in use until the 1960s.

In 1868, five years after Freeman filed his claim under the Homestead Act, he received the title to his land as promised. Freeman died in 1908 and is buried on his property, now a national landmark to honor and remember those pioneers who helped grow America under the Homestead Act.

CAPITAL POLITICS

1868

The horses were saddled and ready to go. They stomped their feet on the frozen ground and shook the gathering snow from their tails. Nearby, a group of men huddled close together to ward off the cold. It was late in the evening on a snowy December 1868 day in Omaha, Nebraska.

The men were about to do something drastic. The Nebraska Legislature had approved a bill to move the state's capital from Omaha to the newly established town of Lincoln about fifty miles to the southwest. However, many state officials, including Governor David Butler, didn't believe the citizens of Omaha would let the capital go. Omaha had served as the capital since the territory was established in 1854 and liked it. Now Nebraska was a state and had been for nearly two years. Even though the bill to move the capital had passed in May of 1867, nothing had been done in Omaha to prepare for the move.

Things had progressed in Lincoln. A capitol building had been quickly erected during the past few months and city officials were in talks with Burlington Railroad to establish a line to the community.

The men huddled by the horses received the all-clear sign. One by one, they entered the brick building by a small back door and made their way through the structure. For the next few hours, the men silently worked to clear a certain room of documents and artifacts relating to the governing of Nebraska. By midnight, the room was empty and the horses were loaded down.

Without attracting any undue attention, the men led their horses to the edge of town. There they met another group of men and fresh horses. Mounting the new horses, the men turned their backs on Omaha and began the long ride back to Lincoln, leading the pack horses.

With them they took the state's capital. All of the paperwork, including deeds and certificates, mysteriously disappeared from the old capitol in Omaha that night and just as mysteriously turned up in Lincoln in the new capitol building.

Within a month, the Nebraska legislature would meet again, this time in Lincoln. The change was made.

This midnight ride through a snowstorm with "stolen" papers is just the kind of controversy that was not new to Nebraska. In April 1864, the US Congress gave the okay to the Nebraska territorial government to create a state constitution. The state's Democrats and Republicans had a hard time agreeing on anything and the constitution was approved by a margin of only one hundred votes. Two years later, Nebraskans voted for their first governor. David Butler beat out J. Sterling Morton by, again, one hundred votes. Charges of voter fraud in both cases abounded, but nothing was ever proved.

In December of 1866, the United States Congress passed the resolution naming Nebraska as the country's thirty-seventh state, effective March 1, 1867. However, President Andrew Johnson was opposed to the statehood and vetoed the bill. Congress overrode Johnson's veto, the only time in the country's history that a statehood bill became law over a presidential veto.

Then came the question of where to have the capital. Omaha citizens, of course, wanted to keep the capital there. When they heard rumors that a site in Lancaster County was being looked at as a place for the new capital, they decided to name the area Lincoln after President Abraham Lincoln. The thought was that Democrats in the area would not support a capital named after the Republican president. That idea backfired and Lincoln was chosen as the new capital.

After the capital was firmly established in Lincoln, paperwork and all, things were still not all smooth sailing. The first capitol building built in Lincoln cost twice as much as originally estimated and began to fall apart immediately after occupation. The structure built to replace it wasn't much better. Lincoln was still a fledgling community with no railroad service and no river access. Finally, in 1871, Governor Butler was impeached for misappropriating funds in a scheme that revealed he illegally purchased lots in Lincoln to pad the number of constituents in the small community.

Things settled down in Nebraska after that. Burlington Railroad came to town and a university was established close to the capital. In the 1920s, a new capitol building was designed and erected at a cost of nearly ten million dollars. It was included on the National Register of Historic Places in 1970 and became a National Historic Landmark in 1976. It is still used as the capitol today.

In 1934, Nebraska voters approved a plan to move to a nonpartisanship unicameral system of government. The change was implemented in 1937. Nebraska remains the only nonpartisan or unicameral system of government in the United States.

A GIFT FOR THE FUTURE

1872

Julius Sterling Morton re-read the final draft of the document before
him. Nodding to himself, he picked up his pen, dipped the nub into
a waiting bottle of ink, and scratched his name on the bottom of the
page. Sighing, Morton pushed back his chair and stood, stretching
out the kinks in his back. He walked over to the window and pushed
aside the lace curtain.

Morton stared out at a snowy landscape, but his mind was
picturing the upcoming spring. It was December 1871 and Morton
had just finished preparing a document he wanted to present to the
Nebraska legislature after the start of the new year. In this document,
Morton was requesting the lawmakers set aside a day each April for
tree-planting. Morton was hoping the idea would take "root" in the
new state.

Morton had arrived in the Nebraska territory in 1854 and settled
in Nebraska City in 1855. Although only twenty-two years of age,
Morton was employed as editor of the *Nebraska City News,* one
of the territory's first newspapers. Morton and his wife, Caroline,

homesteaded in Nebraska from Michigan and the lack of trees on the prairie was a concern to the couple. The Mortons built a four-room frame house on the edge of Nebraska City and began planting trees and shrubs on their property.

Morton used his position at the *Nebraska City News* to encourage other settlers to the area to plant trees. At a Horticultural Society meeting in Lincoln in the early 1870s, he stated, "There is beauty in a well ordered orchard which is a 'joy forever.' . . . If I had the power I would compel every man in the State who had a home of his own, to plant out and cultivate fruit trees."

Nebraska was the start of what was then called the Great American Desert. Major Stephen H. Long, on the first government-sponsored expedition across the Midwest in 1820, had coined the phrase by simply writing it across the vast expanse of prairie depicted on his map. Long did not provide many other details about the plains and the image of a forbidding desert remained.

When Morton and his bride arrived in Nebraska, the only trees that grew were small cottonwoods and bur oaks on the banks of streams and rivers. Morton knew that if the state wanted to entice settlers, they would need to create comfortable neighborhoods and tree-lined downtowns. With that in mind, Morton had drafted his resolution.

On January 4, 1872, Morton attended a meeting of the Nebraska State Board of Agriculture and presented his idea of setting aside one day each spring for tree-planting throughout the state. He called it Arbor Day.

The State Board of Agriculture unanimously approved the resolution and four months later, on April 10, 1872, Nebraskans planted one million trees across the state. Morton himself had ordered eight hundred trees to plant on his property in Nebraska City, but, in a strange twist of fate, those trees did not arrive on time and Morton was forced to wait to take part in the celebration.

Morton and his family kept planting year after year and soon developed a thriving apple orchard, which became the largest apple orchard in the Midwest by the 1920s. As the years went by, more states began observing Arbor Day annually, and it is now celebrated in all fifty states and across the world.

Morton had no way of knowing that his simple proclamation would garner such interest nationwide. He was working with the idea of doing good for the earth and the people who were going to live in the area. But perhaps Morton was a bit prophetic; he said it best when he stated, "Arbor Day is not like other holidays. Each of those reposes on the past, while Arbor Day proposes for the future."

MASSACRE CANYON

1873

The story of Massacre Canyon is not a pretty one. It is filled with blood and death. It is based in politics, aggression, and ignorance. It could have been avoided and it wholly illustrates the mismanagement of relations with Native Americans by the white man.

The story starts generations before 1873. Thousands of years before European explorers and settlers came to the Midwest, the Pawnee and Sioux Indian tribes populated the area. They did not live together in peace, but rather had a violent relationship filled with skirmishes and battles over land and food. When the white settlers moved into the plains and tried to govern the Native Americans they found there, the settlers ignored years of strife and hatred and grouped different tribes together, often forcing them off their ancestral land. Years before, the Pawnee had aligned themselves with the white man in order to survive, but years of disease and fighting with the Sioux had taken their toll. By 1873, there were very few Pawnee left.

One staple of Pawnee life was the buffalo hunt. The Pawnee would follow buffalo herds throughout the plains, often up to five hundred miles from their villages. However, once the Pawnee were under the government's watch, the buffalo hunts were restricted. During the summer of 1873, Pawnee leaders had arranged to go on a sanctioned buffalo hunt in southwest Nebraska. A white trail agent, John William Williamson, accompanied 350 Pawnee on the hunt.

Williamson, at the young age of twenty-three, was not prepared to advise the Pawnee. He was a fairly new trail agent and had not been on the plains much. In July of that summer, Williamson and the Pawnee came across a group of white buffalo hunters following the same herd. The hunters, aware of the bloody history between the Pawnee and the Sioux, warned the Pawnee that a band of Sioux warriors was also in area. The Pawnee were suspicious of the hunters' motives and chose not to believe the warnings. Williamson tried to convince the Pawnee to turn back from the hunt, but his arguments fell on deaf ears. The Pawnee were sure the white hunters wanted the buffalo all to themselves. Williamson could not change their minds and the hunt continued.

Williamson, in his inexperience, was also unable to convince the Pawnee to send out scouts to patrol the area. The Pawnee continued tracking the buffalo and found a portion of the herd in a small canyon near what is now Trenton, Nebraska. It was August 5, 1873.

A group of hunters led the Pawnee into the canyon. Behind the hunters were the women and children of the tribe, carrying meat already acquired and supplies for the hunt. As the Pawnee advanced, suddenly more than one thousand Sioux Indians appeared on the rim of the canyon, weapons drawn. The Pawnee were trapped!

Without warning, the Sioux began raining arrows down on the Pawnee in the canyon. The hunters who had led the group were the first to fall.

Williamson knew he had to do something. He rode out in front of the Pawnee and attempted to broker a truce with the Sioux. As an answer, the Sioux shot Williamson's horse out from under him. Williamson ran back to the main group of Pawnee while the fighting continued.

In the chaos that ensued, the Pawnees attempted to retreat back the way they had come. Those carrying supplies and food dropped their loads and ran for their lives. The Sioux continued to advance, striking those at the rear of the fleeing tribe. Once the last of the Pawnee exited the canyon, the Sioux halted the attack and began to gather the dropped food and supplies left by the Pawnee.

In the meantime, the Pawnee continued to run. Williamson led what was left of the tribe to a nearby army encampment. There Williamson spoke with Captain Charles Meinhold and told him of the massacre. Meinhold led a group of soldiers to the canyon, but the Sioux were long gone. What the soldiers found instead were the bloodied remains of seventy Pawnee killed in the attack. Twenty of the fallen were men and the rest were women and children.

According to reports from the incident, the army did try to find the band of Sioux warriors who attacked the Pawnee, but they were unsuccessful. A soldier assigned to work with the Sioux, in the same capacity as Williamson had worked with the Pawnee, later reported that only six Sioux died in the fight, compared with the seventy Pawnee lost.

The Pawnee never went on another buffalo hunt, and within three years, all were moved to the Oklahoma Indian territory to live on a reservation. The event at what is now called Massacre Canyon is believed to have been one of the last altercations between two major Native American tribes of the Midwest. The Sioux and the Pawnee, mortal enemies for centuries, did not meet in battle again.

GRASSHOPPER INVASION

1874

The summer of 1874 was hot and dry in Nebraska. The Midwest was experiencing a drought and farmers were worried about their crops. On one bright Sunday morning in late July, clouds began to build on the horizon. Farmers were relieved, thinking a soaking rain was coming.

However, the clouds moved in at an incredible speed and it wasn't long before farmers realized that what they mistook for clouds was really a mass of insects. Jumping and flying grasshoppers. Billions of them, roaring like a storm.

Within minutes, swarms of grasshoppers covered every square inch of crops. The drought conditions actually helped the insects in their quest for food; most prairie plants store extra sugars in their stalks during drought times, so the grasshoppers had plenty to eat.

Grasshoppers not only covered the crops, but they also alit on any other surface they could find. Millions at a time would settle on tree branches, their weight causing the branches to snap. More would get caught under heavy train wheels, dying by the thousands.

Soon, railroad tracks were slick with grasshopper guts and the trains couldn't get enough traction to move.

The invasion in 1874 lasted only a few days, but when the grasshoppers left Nebraska, the farmers didn't have to worry about their crops anymore. No crops survived.

The invasion had far-reaching repercussions. Not only were the crops devastated that year, but more grasshoppers came in the following years, hatched from eggs laid during the 1874 invasion. Farm animals innocently ate grasshoppers by the ton, which in some cases caused the death of those animals and in other cases left those animals inedible to humans.

Many farmers gave up after the grasshopper invasions, moving out of Nebraska for good. Some were homesteaders, who were required to work the land for five years. They relinquished their claims and let the land go wild.

Today, tales of grasshopper invasions are regarded as myths. The people of Nebraska in 1874 would testify otherwise.

BIG SPRINGS ROBBERY

1877

The "Black Hills Bandits," as they were known, were bored. They had spent the last few months robbing stagecoach after stagecoach and had yet to hit the big one. Robbing stagecoaches seemed to be just small potatoes.

Sam Bass was the leader of the Black Hills Bandits. The twenty-six-year-old outlaw had grown up in Indiana and had spent the last few years traveling all over the United States in search of an easy way to get rich. His five companions in the Black Hills Bandits gang pretty much shared the same story: troubled and poor childhoods, no luck with stable and legal careers, turning to lives of gambling and crime.

Sam and his gang were wandering around western Nebraska in the fall of 1877 when they came upon a bright idea. The Union Pacific line went across the entire state of Nebraska, following the Platte River. The trains had water stops set up along the route and Sam figured they could take advantage of that. The Black Hills Bandits were going to attempt to rob a Union Pacific train, a feat that had never been done before.

In the early 1860s, Union Pacific decided to locate its headquarters in Omaha. Beginning in 1865 at the end of the Civil War, tracks were laid east to west across the state. At first, workers could lay one mile of track per day, but they soon increased production. The track was completed in 1869.

Towns began to spring up every twenty miles or so along the completed track. Some towns turned into large cities, while others floundered. One of the water stops along the route was in Big Springs, Nebraska, twenty miles west of Ogallala. Big Springs was not an incorporated town; it consisted of a railroad station and a few houses. It did have a fresh spring nearby, which gave the town its name.

Everything went according to plan for Sam Bass and his gang. On the evening of September 18, 1877, they broke into the Big Springs train station, severely beat up stationmaster John Barnhart, and destroyed the station's telegraph machine. The break-in coincided with the eleven o'clock arrival of the Union Pacific Express Train Number 4. Forcing the passenger train to stop, the gang boarded and went through the train cars one by one, relieving the passengers of money, jewelry, and watches. That alone added up to more than one thousand dollars in booty.

However, that thousand dollars paled in comparison to what else the Bandits found. Stacked neatly in strong wooden boxes were piles of bright gold coins, newly minted in San Francisco. Each coin was a twenty-dollar gold piece. The stash added up to sixty thousand dollars!

Sam and the Black Hills Bandits took off with their loot and hid. The money and coins were split up between the six men and they all went their different ways. A couple of them disappeared and a few were caught and killed. Sam Bass himself was shot dead less than a year later in Round Rock, Texas.

The Big Springs Robbery was the first and biggest train robbery in Union Pacific history. None of the money stolen was ever recovered and some speculate Sam Bass may have hidden his share somewhere between Big Springs and Round Rock.

I AM A MAN

1879

Standing Bear lifted the shovel and turned over a fresh patch of dark earth. He dug into the ground again and again. With each push of the shovel, Standing Bear thought of his past and the journey that brought him to this place and time.

He was high in the bluffs above the confluence of the Missouri River and the Niobrara River in northeast Nebraska. This was the Ponca ancestral land where Standing Bear had been born and raised like generations of his people before him, but it had taken years of legal work and thousands of miles traveled for him to stand here now.

As the grave he dug grew wider and deeper, Standing Bear thought of all the treaties his people had signed with the US government, beginning in 1817. With each treaty, four in all for the Ponca, more land had been given to the government and more promises had been made and broken by the government.

Standing Bear didn't know that the United States had signed 374 different treaties with various Indian tribes over the course of one hundred years, and he didn't know of the 1868 Treaty of Fort Laramie in particular. That treaty had mistakenly ceded the Ponca land to their enemy, the Lakota. The error was never corrected and, more important, no one had ever notified the Ponca of the mistake.

From 1868 until 1877, the Lakota became more aggressive in their attacks on the Ponca, who appealed to the government for help and protection. In 1877, on a cold January day, a government Indian agent finally appeared in the Ponca village. He informed the tribe of the change in ownership of the land and told the Ponca they were now instructed to pack up all their belongings and move to the Indian Territory, located in what is now Oklahoma, hundreds of miles to the south.

The news shocked the Ponca. They had lived on this land for hundreds of years and their ancestors were buried in the rich soil of the hills above the river. How could they be expected to leave?

Standing Bear was an honored tribal chief and was recognized most often by the bear claw necklace he wore. In 1877, he was nearing fifty and had a family and tribe he loved. The Ponca only numbered about five hundred; years of disease and warfare had taken their toll on the peaceful people. Standing Bear didn't want to move his people, but he also didn't want to fight.

All the chiefs of the tribe met and decided to go along with the Indian agent to view the Indian Territory. In their minds, if they didn't find a place they liked and could make into a home, they would be allowed to come back to Nebraska. In the mind of the Indian agent, they were going to the Indian Territory to stay.

As Standing Bear turned over the earth on that hot late summer afternoon, he recalled that first trip to the Indian Territory. The Indian agent took them south first in wagons and then by train. From their first glimpse of the new territory, the Ponca chiefs were not impressed. Their home in Nebraska was filled with gently rolling hills of green grass and deep blue waters. The Indian Territory in Oklahoma was flat and arid, with a rocky soil unsuitable for farming. Standing Bear and his fellow chiefs told the Indian agent they refused to settle there, but the Indian agent was already making plans to bring the rest of the tribe down to join them. Realizing that arguing with the government man was futile, Standing Bear and the other chiefs slipped out of their hotel and headed for home.

Standing Bear stopped his digging and lifted his head to stare out over the river. That winter trip back north was the first of many times he would end up walking the six hundred miles that separated the Ponca lands from the Indian Territory. He remembered the cold and fatigue. He also remembered the kindness of strangers who offered the ragged band of Indians food and shelter along the way.

When Standing Bear and the other chiefs reached home a couple of months later, they found the removal of the tribe was already under way. They again attempted to argue with the Indian agent; he had taken the train back north and had gotten to the Ponca tribe before the chiefs made it back. The Indian agent brought something new with him this time—a military detachment.

In May of 1877, under the watchful eye of the military, the Ponca tribe loaded down wagons with all their personal goods and turned south. Now, over the open grave, Standing Bear closed his eyes in grief when he thought of that trip. Six hundred miles on foot, suffering from disease, cold rains, a tornado, swollen creeks, washed out roads, and finally, when they reached the Indian Territory, an oppressive heat unlike anything they had ever felt in northeastern Nebraska. Every day on the trek south someone would fall ill and many died and were buried along the way, including Standing Bear's own daughter. The Ponca people wailed in sorrow the entire way, grieving the loss of their people and their land. The route they took became known as the Ponca Trail of Tears.

The Indian agent said things would be better in the Indian Territory, but they weren't. There was no housing or shelter at all for the Ponca tribe and no plants or crops had been planted. Now it was past planting season and the Indians began to waste away from starvation. In addition, many contracted malaria. With no immunity to this type of sickness, dozens of Ponca died in their first year in the Indian Territory. By the winter of 1878, a quarter of the tribe was dead.

Among the dead was a young Ponca named Bear Shield. The teenager was Standing Bear's only son. On his deathbed, he asked his father to take him back north and bury him on the ancestral lands. Standing Bear agreed.

Standing Bear looked down at the grave beneath his feet. His son had died more than six months ago, but Standing Bear could still see his face, swollen with sickness. He could hear his son's shaky whisper begging his father to take him home. Standing Bear could also remember the determination he felt to do just that.

Accompanied by twenty-nine of his family members and fellow Ponca Indians, Standing Bear snuck away from their land on the Indian Territory, bringing the body of Bear Shield with him. It was January 1879. It took the Ponca Indian agent a few weeks to notice the small band was missing from the Indian Territory, but once he did, he immediately sent telegrams north, warning government officials that the Indians did not have permission to be off their land in Oklahoma. It was April 1879 by the time Standing Bear crossed into Nebraska and led his family to the lands of the Omaha Indian tribe, where they were met by a troop of Army soldiers.

Leading the soldiers was Civil War veteran and West Point Military Academy graduate Brigadier General George Crook, Commander of the Department of the Platte. Crook took the Poncas to Fort Crook near the city of Omaha and put them in jail.

Standing Bear smiled when he thought of his friend George Crook. It was thanks to Crook that Standing Bear was where he was today, a free man, free to dig a grave for his son.

Crook was obeying orders when he arrested Standing Bear, but he didn't like it. In recent years, Crook had become disenchanted with the government's treatment of Indians and was looking for a way to change things. That night, after interning the Poncas at Fort Omaha, General Crook paid a visit to Thomas Tibbles at the *Omaha Daily Herald.*

Crook told Tibbles about Standing Bear and his troubles with the government. Tibbles, assistant editor at the paper, understood what Crook wanted him to do and set to work. On April 1, 1879, the *Omaha Daily Herald* ran an editorial about the plight of the Ponca. Tibbles telegraphed that same story, and many others in the days that followed, to various papers on the East Coast. He was stirring the public's interest in the affair and hoping to gain sympathy for Indian rights.

Tibbles did something else on the recommendation of Crook. Presenting the issue of the arrest before two Omaha attorneys, John Webster and Andrew Poppleton, Tibbles asked if they would fight on behalf of Standing Bear against the US government on the grounds of the Fourteenth Amendment, which had been enacted a decade before in response to the issue of black rights at the end of the Civil War. It guaranteed US citizens equal protection under the law. Would Webster and Poppleton argue that Standing Bear was not being offered the rights due to him as a citizen?

Webster and Poppleton took the case. They filed the suit in federal court. *Standing Bear v. Crook* went before Judge Elmer S. Dundy on May 1, 1879. Even though General Crook was named as the defendant in the case, he came to the trial dressed in full military regalia to argue on the side of Standing Bear. Crook knew the only way to change the government's actions toward Indians was by getting a federal ruling on the issue.

There was standing room only in the Omaha courtroom on May 1. The Ponca who accompanied Standing Bear to the north appeared in their ragged clothing, but Standing Bear himself was garbed in full Ponca dress, beaded and colorful.

Judge Dundy heard testimony and arguments from both sides that first day. On May 2, 1879, closing arguments began at ten o'clock in the morning. Webster and Poppleton argued that under the Fourteenth Amendment, Standing Bear should be treated like any other American. They said the US government had wrongly given away the Ponca lands and had no right to force the tribe to move to the Indian Territory. They further argued that the current jailing of the tribal members at Fort Omaha was against the law.

The defense attorney took the floor next and spoke his piece, saying Indians were not entitled to rights or privileges of citizenship. The defense attorney cited the *Dred Scott* decision of 1857, which ruled that blacks could not be considered citizens. Webster and Poppleton countered that argument by stating the Fourteenth Amendment, which went into an effect in 1868, nullified *Dred Scott*.

The closing arguments ended at ten o'clock in the evening on May 2, a full twelve hours after they began. Before dismissing the courtroom, Judge Dundy gave Standing Bear permission to speak one last time. Standing Bear stood, faced the crowded courtroom, and began: "This hand is not the color of yours, but if I pierce it, I shall feel pain. If you pierce your hand, you also feel pain. The blood that will flow from mine will be of the same color as yours. I am a man. The same God made us both."

Ten days later, on May 12, 1879, Judge Dundy released his decision. According to his reading of the law, "an Indian is a person within the meaning of the law." Dundy went on to say Crook had no grounds to imprison Standing Bear and the Ponca.

The decision was printed in full in the May 13, 1879, edition of the *Omaha Daily Herald.* It marked the first time in the history of the United States that Indians were given any public recognition in the court system. One week later, Standing Bear and his family left the barracks at Fort Omaha and headed north.

Two more months passed before Standing Bear was able to bury his son as he had promised. Even though the Ponca were free, their ancestral land still officially belonged to the Lakota. It took some time for Standing Bear and his tribe to find an uninhabited island in the Niobrara River that was outside of the Lakota area and to settle there. Even though the surrounding land now belonged to the Lakota, members of that tribe had no interest in living there, so the Ponca were alone.

Standing Bear put down his shovel. The events of the past flowed through his mind like the Niobrara below him. Standing Bear had relinquished many of his Indian ways. He had given away his beaded buckskin leggings to the journalist Tibbles and now wore a shirt and trousers like the white man. His tomahawk went to the lawyer Webster and Standing Bear now wielded a plow. His most sacred object, an ancestral headdress thought to be several hundreds of years old, was given to the lawyer Poppleton and would no longer adorn the brow of the Ponca chief.

But Standing Bear still wore his bear claw necklace, and still knew the ceremonial rites that would send his son into the spirit world. That day, he fulfilled his promise to his dying son and laid him to rest with his ancestors.

The story of Standing Bear does not end with his son's burial. Tibbles resigned his post at the *Omaha Daily Herald* and started a speaking tour in the East. The tour was designed to raise funds and awareness about Indian rights. Tibbles's main focus was on lawsuits filed in federal courts in Nebraska and the Dakota Territory aimed at giving the Ponca back their land. Standing Bear joined Tibbles on his tour and became a well-known figure. He told his story to packed houses again and again.

By the time the federal court ruled that the Ponca could legally have back their ancestral lands in 1890, the thirty Ponca who had accompanied Standing Bear to Nebraska in 1879 had grown to two hundred. They resettled in their homeland and wrote to the Ponca who had stayed behind in the Indian Territory. Did they want to come home as well?

The southern tribe of Ponca debated returning to Nebraska, but things had changed for them. The sickness that had taken so many in the first few years had leveled off and the Ponca were learning to live off the harsh land of the Indian Territory. They decided to stay in the South.

As for Standing Bear himself, he found a section of fertile land near the river he loved and successfully farmed his property until his death in 1908. He was buried alongside his ancestors and his son, high on the green hills of northeast Nebraska.

BUFFALO BILL CODY RIDES AGAIN

1883

"Buffalo Bill's Wild West and Congress of Rough Riders of the World." The bearded man held the advertisement out in front of him and squinted. His eyes took in the illustration of bare-chested Indians on horseback and sharp-shooting cowboys taking aim. "You don't think it's too much, do you?"

Louisa Cody put down her knitting and looked at the poster held out to her by her husband. She smiled. "I think it's perfect," she said.

The Codys were in their living room in North Platte, Nebraska, sitting in front of the fireplace on a cold winter night. Buffalo Bill was perusing documents received that day regarding the production of his new Wild West Combination. The show was set to open across the state in Omaha in May of 1883, just a few months away.

Buffalo Bill was sure his Wild West Combination was going to be a success. Off and on for the last fifty or so years, cowboys in the American frontier had gotten together once or twice a year to compete in informal contests of skill and daring. These contests were known as rodeos. Just last year, in honor of North Platte's

Independence Day of 1882, Buffalo Bill himself had taken that idea and organized what he called the Old Glory Blowout, featuring skilled horseback riders, sharpshooters, and even real Indians dressed in their finery. The crowd had loved it. Now, Buffalo Bill was expanding his Old Glory Blowout and adding knife throwers, live buffalo, and even a reenactment of Custer's Last Stand. He was going to bring the romance of the American West to the big city.

Buffalo Bill knew his audience. For over ten years, Buffalo Bill had worked as an actor on the stage, usually portraying himself. He would reenact scenes from his life, including, of course, buffalo hunting.

Buffalo Bill had been born William F. Cody in eastern Iowa in 1846. His family moved to Kansas when he was a youngster, but tragedy struck. Cody's father, a fierce abolitionist, was stabbed after giving an anti-slavery speech and soon died from the wounds. Cody, at age eleven, was the now the head of his household. He went to work as an ox team driver and began to travel the plains. In 1860, at age fourteen, Cody signed on with the freighting company of Russell, Majors, and Waddell to be a Pony Express rider. When the Civil War erupted, Cody tried to enlist, but was turned away for being too young. The Union Army did allow Cody to work for them as a scout and a teamster, hauling supplies from fort to fort.

After the war, Cody took a job with the Kansas Pacific Railroad. For the salary of five hundred dollars a month, Cody was to provide buffalo meat for the railroad's employees. Cody earned his nickname, "Buffalo Bill," after reportedly killing four thousand buffalo in eight months.

In 1872, Cody earned international fame when he agreed to guide the Grand Duke Alexis of Russia on a hunting trip through the western United States. The trip was a well-publicized event. The following year, Cody started work as an actor. The job had allowed him to purchase a cattle ranch just north of North Platte. That's where he was now, planning his next big adventure.

Buffalo Bill knew the public was anxious to see a dramatization of life on the plains. He had cowboys lined up to do trick horseback riding and had written reenactments of his time as a Pony Express rider. There would be acts of showmanship and a parade of some of the finest horses this side of the Mississippi River, along with a menagerie of wild animals.

The Wild West and Congress of Rough Riders of the World was a commercial and critical success for Buffalo Bill from day one. After wowing crowds in Omaha, Buffalo Bill and his troupe toured the Eastern Seaboard and, by 1887, had attracted international attention as well. That year, joined by female sharpshooter Annie Oakley and the Lakota Sioux Sitting Bull, Buffalo Bill took his show to England for Queen Victoria's Golden Jubilee, which marked her fiftieth year of rule. In 1900, Buffalo Bill partnered with James A. Bailey of Barnum and Bailey Circus fame and his show grew even larger and featured more unique and exotic animals and exhibitions.

During the peak of popularity for his Wild West, Buffalo Bill's dream of having a sprawling place of his own was realized. In 1886, Buffalo Bill purchased four thousand acres of Nebraska land adjacent to his North Platte–area ranch. The land was mostly sand hills, which suited Buffalo Bill's needs perfectly. He built an eighteen-room mansion for himself and his family and a large barn to house his animals and equipment when Wild West wasn't touring. The sand hills provided excellent grazing lands for the horses and cattle. Naming the ranch "Scouts Rest," Buffalo Bill used the property as an escape in between tours.

Buffalo Bill's Wild West endured until into the twentieth century, but changes in management and a decline in popularity forced its closure in 1913. Buffalo Bill died in 1917, but the ideals of the American West that he portrayed live on in books, film, and organized rodeos across the country.

SCHOOLCHILDREN'S BLIZZARD

1888

The schoolhouse hummed with activity as the students settled down to do their work. It was early in the day on Thursday, January 12, 1888, and their teacher, Minnie May Freeman, had assigned each grade level a special project to do while she cleaned. Minnie had walked the half-mile distance from her boarding house in Ord to the sod school building that morning in high spirits. After nearly a week of bitterly cold temperatures, the day had dawned gloriously warm by January standards, and Minnie was going to allow the students to play outside for a bit later in the day.

Minnie swept the snow that had been tracked in by the children out the front door and leaned against the doorframe, watching her students work. The one-room schoolhouse was warm and cozy, but Minnie noticed she was getting low on fuel near the stove. She made a mental note to replenish the fuel the next day.

The rest of the morning passed uneventfully. Minnie helped the younger students with their numbers, while the older students worked on geography. Minnie, who was not much older than some of her oldest students, appreciated that her classroom could run efficiently even with so many students learning at so many different levels.

As promised, Minnie let the students out early for lunch to give them extra time to play outside. Several of the students walked to their homes for lunch, returning quickly to be with their friends. At precisely one o'clock, Minnie called the students into the schoolhouse.

As the students settled into their seats, the sod schoolhouse rapidly darkened. Minnie headed to one of the windows in the side of the building and peered outside into the sudden gloom. She gasped.

Where there had been bright sunshine just before was now a mass of white moving across the landscape at unbelievable speed. Minnie had never before seen such a quick-moving storm. Within minutes, the schoolhouse was consumed by the blizzard.

Temperatures fell dramatically in the sod building. Minnie moved to the stove and then stopped, remembering she had used up all her fuel earlier in the day. Turning to face her students, she smiled bravely.

"Well, this is unexpected!" she said brightly. "Let's wait a bit and see if the storm will lessen any."

What Minnie did not realize was the storm had been gathering speed for over twenty-four hours, moving swiftly across the Dakotas and into Nebraska at forty-five miles per hour. The temperatures statewide went from the upper thirties to negative forty degrees in some places in less than a few hours. Soon the entire state was in the grip of the blizzard.

❧

Two hours later, the temperature in the sod schoolhouse had continued to drop; the fire in the stove was now only smoldering. Minnie and her students were huddled together, dressed in coats and scarves and gloves, playing word games to pass the time. Some of the younger students began to cry. The storm outside raged without ceasing, the wind shrieking and howling.

A groaning sound came from the roof of the sod schoolhouse. The students yelled as a portion of the roof slowly tore back from the walls of the building, exposing the interior to the ferocious storm outside.

Minnie grabbed for her students as the snow and wind swirled around them. She knew something had to be done.

Lois May Royce, a teacher in a small schoolhouse near Plainview, had also been caught unaware. She had three small children with her that day. Lois's boardinghouse was less than two hundred feet away, although she could not see it in the blizzard. Lois gathered her charges and set out for home, thinking they would make it there in a matter of minutes.

Minnie pushed her students under the small portion of the roof that remained and watched as the rest of her classroom was swallowed in snow. It was now below freezing and she knew they couldn't stay here. Pulling aside the older students, she outlined her plan. They nodded and began to form the students into a line, having each child grasp the hands of the people on either side of him or her. The human chain worked its way to the main door of the schoolhouse, with Minnie in the lead.

Minnie took her bearings in the now ruined schoolhouse and squared her shoulders toward what she hoped was her boardinghouse. She knew she would have to be sure about which direction she was heading, or she would lead her students out onto the prairie with no shelter awaiting them. Pulling her scarf over her face, Minnie led her students into the heart of the storm.

Lois had miscalculated. They had been walking for what seemed like hours in the whiteout and had yet to find her boardinghouse, or any structure for that matter. The three little ones she was shepherding were numb with cold and fatigue. Lois tripped and stumbled into a haystack.

I'll just settle down in here with the children, *she thought.* Just until we get warm. *Lois pulled apart the haystack and helped the three students inside. She slipped in after them, trying to pull the hay around her.*

Minnie didn't know how long they had been walking, heads bowed under the weight of the blizzard. With the sound of the wind roaring in their ears, there was no way to talk to her students, to make sure they were all okay and still holding on. Holding back tears of exhaustion, Minnie walked on.

Lois couldn't feel her legs anymore. One of the students had fallen asleep and Lois couldn't get her to wake up. The other two were crying bitterly. Lois squirmed in the haystack and waited for the storm to abate.

Suddenly, a large structure loomed out of the darkness before Minnie. Reaching out with one hand, she touched the side of a house. It was her boardinghouse! They had made it! Carefully, Minnie led her students around the house to the front porch. One by one, they squeezed through the front door and into warmth and safety. Not a single student was lost.

Minnie Freeman was hailed as a hero for saving her students. The storm ended the next morning, shutting off as suddenly as it had come up. The storm caught Nebraskans by surprise as they worked outside or were at school. Some teachers burned desks and chairs to keep warm. Others kept their students all night until the storm blew itself out. Livestock were casualties too, although there are many stories of horses and cows instinctively finding their way home in the blizzard, often leading their owners to safety.

Lois Royce and her three students were found the next day in a haystack. The three children died; Lois's legs had to be amputated.

Hundreds of Nebraskans lost their lives in the storm. The exact number was never properly recorded. In all the records of storms that came before and since, none have measured up to be as terrible as the Blizzard of 1888.

FLIPPIN PLAYS FOOTBALL

1892

In the whole scheme of the country, Nebraska is not known for its role in the fight for civil rights for African Americans. No Civil War battles were fought on her soil; no freedom marches were advanced in her capital. Aside from a few negative occurrences, Nebraska has quietly and consistently supported the rights of blacks.

Never is that better illustrated than in the story of George Flippin. While most readers may be unfamiliar with the name of George Flippin, almost all will be familiar with what he did: play football at the University of Nebraska.

Football and Nebraska are closely intertwined, especially during the fall months. The tradition of a university team playing the game in the plains began in 1890. That year, the team only played two games, winning both.

The highlight of this story occurs one chilly fall morning in November of 1892, but it begins a generation before with George's father, Charles.

Charles Flippin fought in the Civil War in the Union's 14th US Colored Troops Company A. Charles was a freed slave. After the war, Charles attended the Bennett Eclectic Medical School in Chicago, Illinois, and became a doctor. He moved to Henderson and then to Stromsburg, practicing medicine in both small Nebraska towns.

Charles was ahead of his time. Not only did he, a former slave, attend medical school, but after his wife died, he married a white women who was also a doctor. Charles and his second wife both practiced medicine in Nebraska. He encouraged his son to pursue higher education.

George attended the University of Nebraska from 1891 to 1894 and has the honor of being the first black football player for the university. He also played baseball, ran track, and wrestled.

Even though Flippin was a football star on the gridiron, troubles followed him off the field, simply because of the color of his skin. In October of 1892, the Nebraska team traveled to Denver to play the Denver Athletic Club. The players went as a group to an opera house, but Flippin was denied admission. His fellow players walked out of the opera house without a second thought. During that same trip, Flippin was not allowed in the hotel dining room. In solidarity, his teammates refused to eat.

In November of 1892, the Nebraska football team was scheduled to head to Omaha and meet with the Missouri Tigers for a game. Nebraska and Missouri, along with the University of Iowa and the University of Kansas, had combined at the beginning of the school year to form the Western Inter-State University Football Association. This game against Missouri was to be Nebraska's first ever conference game.

Flippin was a starting player for the Nebraska Bugeaters, as they were known then. The halfback weighed in at two hundred pounds on his six-foot-two-inch frame. When Missouri found out Flippin was black, they said they would only play Nebraska if Flippin stayed behind in Lincoln. Nebraska refused to leave Flippin on the bench and Missouri forfeited the game. Official scorekeepers entered the final tally as 1-0, Nebraska.

Flippin encountered racism at home in Nebraska as well. He was an excellent player and was well liked by all of his teammates, yet he was never elected captain of the team. In 1894, his last year at the university, Flippin was the players' choice as captain, but the head coach, Frank Crawford, vetoed the vote, saying Flippin was overrated as a player and didn't have the smarts to be captain.

Flippin did have the smarts to be the president of a campus literary society and to continue his education in medical school at the University of Illinois College of Physicians and Surgeons in Chicago. He became a doctor like his father and eventually returned to Stromsburg, Nebraska, to practice. He built a hospital in Stromsburg and continued to practice there until his death in 1929. Flippin was inducted into the Nebraska Football Hall of Fame in 1974.

ORPHAN TRAIN

1899

By the time the Davis twins boarded the train that would take them out of New York City and somewhere west, they had been orphaned two years. Lena and Anna were twelve years old that summer. They had been found selling matches and newspapers on the streets of New York City, trying to survive. The police, instead of arresting Lena and Anna for loitering, took them to the New York Foundling Hospital and recommended they be placed on an orphan train.

Lena and Anna Davis knew they were lucky to be with the New York Foundling Hospital and its sister organization, the Children's Aid Society. They had heard tales of other orphans living on the streets of New York and forming gangs. Often, those children turned to crime and were arrested and placed in jail alongside hardened adult criminals. The prison system was not safe and was becoming overcrowded.

Since the 1850s, the Children's Aid Society and New York Foundling Hospital had been a haven for orphaned, abused, and neglected children. Those children were cleaned up and given a set of new clothes then loaded on a special train. The train took them out of New York City and to states west. Adults waiting for the train would select one or two children to adopt into their family. The children were given a fresh start and a new life.

The train carrying Lena and Anna was scheduled to stop in Nebraska. Lena and Anna had been scared about leaving New York City, the only home they had ever known. They had come to America from Sweden when they were babies, but since their parents died two years before, they had been alone. Lena and Anna didn't even know where Nebraska was when they boarded the train!

The train ride west was uneventful. The Davis twins were careful not to make a mess of their new clothes; they had been told that the people waiting for the orphan train would appreciate nice-looking children.

The majority of the children on the orphan trains were white Christians and no sick or disabled children were allowed. Even though the train carrying Lena and Anna was a normal train, some orphan trains were specially equipped to carry babies. These trains were fitted with quieter wheels, no whistles, and made frequent stops for diaper cloths and fresh milk.

Lena and Anna were jolted awake one morning after about a week on the train. Looking out the window, they spied a sign stating, WELCOME TO GREELEY, NEBRASKA. The train slowed to a halt as it arrived at the small station. Lena and Anna joined the other children waiting on the platform.

A local minister stepped forward and welcomed the children to Greeley. As he moved to the side, the children could see a crowd of adults watching them. Lena nudged Anna in the ribs and they both stood up straighter.

One by one, the adults came forward and looked over the children. One man, whom Lena judged to be a farmer, walked up to a young man about Lena's age and felt his arm muscles through his new shirt. They talked quietly for a minute and then the farmer approached the minister with the boy at his side.

"Excuse me, Reverend," the farmer said. "I'll take this boy. He says his name is Walter. He looks like he'd be a good help to me on the farm."

The minister smiled and nodded, making a note on a piece of paper he held. The farmer and Walter walked to a waiting wagon.

Lena looked up as an older woman approached her. The woman looked her up and down and then glanced over at Anna.

"Are you two twins, then?" the lady asked.

Lena nodded, afraid to speak. She had heard rumors that even though siblings often wanted to stay together, they usually ended up separating and were adopted by different families. The lucky ones we able to at least live in the same town, but Lena had heard of one set of five children who went to five different villages in three different states! She and Anna didn't want to be separated.

As if she knew what Lena was thinking, the lady smiled and put out her hands to both Lena and Anna. "I could use both of you, if you'd like," she said. "I have baby twins at home and I'd like some help in caring for them."

Lena and Anna exchanged hopeful glances. Could they really stay together? Anna spoke first, turning to the lady. "If you please, ma'am, we'd be happy to join your family," she said.

The lady smiled again and turned to the minister. Soon it was all settled. As Lena and Anna were led to a nearby wagon, Lena turned and looked back at the orphan train. There were other children walking away with their new parents, but those who hadn't been chosen were slowly climbing back on the train. They would get off at the next station and be put on display again.

The Davis twins were lucky in their experience with the orphan train. They ended up in a family that loved them, and within the year, their new parents legally adopted both girls. Some members of the orphan train were not so lucky; there are tales of abuse and neglect by the new parents and some children ran away from their new homes and tried to find their way back to New York City.

From the 1850s to the 1920s, an estimated two hundred thousand children were placed on orphan trains and sent throughout the Midwest and Plains states. Most were grateful for the chance to make a better life for themselves and overcame whatever hardships they had lived with in their childhood. These children were given a future.

HAND-PLANTED FOREST

1902

On January 25, 1902, Dr. Charles Edwin Bessey, a professor of botany at the University of Nebraska in Lincoln, sat down at his cluttered desk to write a letter. The letter was addressed to Theodore Roosevelt, the president of the United States of America.

Writing a letter to a government representative was not a new thing, but Bessey was asking President Roosevelt to do something he had never been asked to do before. Bessey, who was originally from Ohio and had studied botany at the Michigan Agriculture College and Harvard University, was proposing that the president set aside a certain portion of land in western Nebraska to be protected as a forest reserve. While there were many forest reserves throughout the nation, this was the first time one was proposed to protect an area of land where there were no actual trees growing . . . yet.

In his letter to President Roosevelt, Bessey emphasized the need to "secure on the open Plains large tracts of land suitable for timber growing." The land Bessey had in mind was in the sand hills of western Nebraska.

Bessey knew trees would grow in the sand hills; in 1891, he had visited Holt County in north central Nebraska and, with permission from the US Department of Agriculture Division of Forestry, started a small forest in the southwest corner of the county. It was in the nature of an experiment in silviculture, which is the art and science of managing trees. Even though the sand hills were free of timber at the time, Bessey and other scientists of his generation were convinced the land had held forests in the distant past and could do so again. Native Nebraska grasses thrived on the sand hills, with their roots stretching deep into the sandy soil beneath them.

Bessey's 1891 planting was controversial. Local ranchers were originally opposed to the idea, fearing a loss of grazing lands. Bessey chose that area of Holt County for the first planting with farmers and ranchers in mind; the land was considered to have poor growing soil, so it was not utilized by local farmers and ranchers. Even though the Division of Forestry initially approved the planting, they did not give Bessey much support and considered the planting to be a waste of time.

Bessey started with 13,500 seedlings planted by hand near Swan Lake in Holt County. However, after that first planting, the Division of Forestry pulled their support for the experiment and funding dried up. Bessey continued his work at the University of Nebraska over the next ten years, teaching classes, developing curricula, and writing textbooks.

Left alone, that small planting in southwest Holt County grew and thrived. By 1901, the trees were twenty feet tall and had filled out to create a dense forest. Bessey had proved a forest could survive in the sand hills of Nebraska.

Bessey's experiment changed the course of Nebraska. Even though the state was becoming more and more settled, the sand hills were still sparse. Bessey knew settlers needed timber for fuel and building, and trees would protect against soil erosion and offer shade and sanctuary. Bessey was the latest of many Nebraskans who advocated tree planting. J. Sterling Morton's Arbor Day Proclamation, adopted by the state legislature in 1872, had done wonders in encouraging tree planting in both urban and rural areas. In 1873, Phineas Hitchcock introduced the Timber Culture Act, which, as a companion to the Homestead Act of 1862, gave homesteaders 160 additional acres of land free if they planted trees on 40 of those acres. Even though the Timber Culture Act was eventually repealed, Nebraska was already known as the Tree Planter's State by the time Bessey pleaded with President Roosevelt to create the forest reserves.

On April 26, 1902, three months after he received Bessey's letter, President Roosevelt created two forest reserves in Nebraska, a 90,000-acre one on the Dismal River near Halsey, and a 124,000-acre tract around the Niobrara River. With the green light to start planting, Bessey and his crew began to plan. By November of 1902, they were ready to plant trees in the forest reserves.

The crew started planting ponderosa pines uprooted from the Pine Ridge country in northwestern Nebraska. Other types of pine and cedar were added to the mix as the reserves grew. Workers dug a well and installed an irrigation system. Turkey and deer, wildlife not normally found in the sand hills, began to appear in the forests. More acres were added to the reserves as the years passed, and in 1906 the North Platte Forest Reserve was included in the protected area with an additional 347,000 acres. The reserves became the Nebraska National Forest in 1907 when Congress created the National Forest system and is the largest hand-planted forest in the United States.

In 1902, when the reserves were first developed, a nursery was built at the Dismal River Reserve to provide seedlings for the other reserve locations. The Charles E. Bessey Nursery became the nation's first federal tree nursery and has provided the other reserves, farmers, and ranchers with millions of seedlings over the years. In 1903, one year after its conception, the Bessey Nursery raised eight hundred thousand seedlings. Twelve years later, in 1915, that number reached 3.3 million. The record number of seedlings, 8.6 million, came in 1941. Currently, the nursery produces up to five million seedlings annually, with over half of those going to Nebraska landowners. Forty species of trees are grown in the nursery.

Local ranchers no longer fight against the plantings; when the forests were laid out, mile-wide sections of bare ground were incorporated into the design. These areas, called fire lanes, help minimize fire impact and local ranchers are encouraged to use the lanes for grazing.

The risk of fire has always been a concern in the Nebraska National Forest. In 1910, fire destroyed many acres of trees before it was brought under control. Another devastating fire occurred in the spring of 1965, killing a third of the forest. Forest managers have simply utilized the bounties of their own nursery in replanting the damaged areas.

Dr. Charles Bessey died in 1915. In his honor, the Dismal River Reserve was renamed the Bessey Ranger District. Bessey's legacy lives on in the sand hills of Nebraska. In his own words, "Let us be true to the name we have adopted of 'Tree-Planter's State.' Plant for shade; plant for protection; plant for beauty; plant for wood; and plant for the conservation of moisture."

BUFFALO SOLDIERS AGAINST THE INDIANS

1906

From its beginnings as an Indian Agency on the White River, Fort Robinson has been tied up with Indian affairs in the American plains. The initial camp started in Wyoming in 1868 as a Red Cloud Indian Agency, designed to provide food and supplies to relocated Indians. In March of 1874 the camp moved near Crawford, Nebraska, in the far northwest corner of the state and was named after Levi H. Robinson, a soldier killed in an Indian attack the month before.

It was the site of the surrender and death of the Sioux warrior Crazy Horse in 1877. The wanted Crazy Horse arrived with nine hundred Oglala Sioux Indians, two thousand horses and mules, and just over one hundred guns on a September afternoon, intent on surrendering to white authorities. During a scuffle with camp soldiers, Crazy Horse was stabbed and died.

A year later, in early winter of 1878, Cheyenne Chief Dull Knife led nearly 150 of his Cheyenne people to Fort Robinson, looking for help. They had fled from the Indian Territory in

Oklahoma and were attempting to make their way back to their homeland. The soldiers at Fort Robinson took them in, fed them and clothed them, then told the Cheyenne they had to go back south to the Indian Territory. The Cheyenne refused and revolted, killing several soldiers. The band of 150 Indians attempted to flee Fort Robinson for the shelter of the nearby bluffs, but nearly half were killed in pursuit, with more dying from cold and hunger in the weeks to come. Of the 150 Cheyenne Indians, only a few were not killed or recaptured by Fort Robinson soldiers to be sent back to the Indian Territory.

The fight against Dull Knife was nearly the end of Indian warfare on the plains, but there was one more instance that involved soldiers of Fort Robinson. This final event also marked the end of military action against Indians in the Plains states.

In 1866, following the Civil War, black men were allowed to form their own units within the US military. The men in these regiments were called Buffalo Soldiers by the Indians they fought. It is believed that the Indians likened the dark skin and curly hair of the black soldiers to that of a buffalo.

Fort Robinson housed two regiments of Buffalo Soldiers from 1885 to 1907. The Ninth Cavalry came to Fort Robinson in 1885 and were instrumental in helping with the expansion of the fort, which began in 1887. At the same time, the railroad was laying tracks to northwest Nebraska and settlers were arriving by the hundreds. The nearby town of Crawford boomed and became known to Fort Robinson soldiers as the place to be when you were off duty. The town boasted many saloons, brothels, and gambling houses, all of which drew the soldiers of Fort Robinson.

For years, Fort Robinson's only neighbors had been Indians and their relationship was tense. Now that towns were springing up, relationships were still tense. This time, it had more to do with the soldiers being black. Even though the Emancipation Proclamation had been in effect for several decades, interactions between blacks and whites remained strained. Fights were common between the white citizens of Crawford and the black soldiers of Fort Robinson and even a few deaths occurred.

Soon, however, tensions eased and the townspeople and soldiers were more cordial to each other. The Ninth Cavalry left Fort Robinson in 1898 and the Tenth Cavalry, also made of Buffalo Soldiers, came in 1902.

The men of the Tenth Cavalry had already seen action in the Battle of San Juan Hill, a crucial battle of the Spanish-American War that was fought in Cuba. They only called Fort Robinson home for eight years, but in 1906, they were involved in the last military action against the Indians.

That year, nearly four hundred Ute Indians fled from their reservation in Utah. They were heading to Montana to find an isolated place in which to settle. The Tenth Cavalry from Fort Robinson was commissioned to round up the Ute Indians and escort them back to Utah.

The event marks a turning point for the American military, and for more reasons than just being the final military act against Indians. Indians at that time, though given equal protection under the law following the Standing Bear trial of 1879, were not US citizens and not offered basic citizenship rights. The Indian Citizenship Act did not become law until 1924, but most were denied basic rights until the passage of the Indian Civil Rights Act of 1968. Blacks were free men, according to the Emancipation Proclamation of 1863, but they also did not have equal rights under the law until the passing of the Civil Rights Act of 1964, which outlawed segregation and discrimination. Both Indians and blacks were minorities in the American society of the time.

The corralling of the Utes marked the end of Indian uprisings on the American plains and the end of Indian interaction with Fort Robinson. The location was basically deserted during World War I, but, beginning in 1919, it was used as a quartermaster remount depot for training and breeding of horses and draft animals for the military. By the late 1930s, Fort Robinson was home to more than fifteen thousand mounts, becoming the largest remount depot in the United States.

The second World War also made use of the space offered by Fort Robinson. From 1942 until 1946, five thousand war dogs were sent to Fort Robinson to receive specialized training, including sentry duty, mine detecting, trail and attack work, and even locating wounded men. Also, additional housing was built at Fort Robinson during that time as the location was deemed prime space to host German prisoners of war, one of several Nebraska locations used for this purpose. Nearly three thousand German soldiers were held at Fort Robinson until after the end of World War II.

In March of 1947, the War Department gave up Fort Robinson and turned the keys over to the Department of Agriculture, and in 1957 it became a state park. It now serves as one of Nebraska's well-loved tourist sites, and newcomers to Fort Robinson are thrilled to learn about Indian raids, Buffalo Soldiers, and more.

THE LITTLE CHURCH OF KEYSTONE

1908

The eleven girls in the front pew of the church could hardly sit still. They fidgeted in their crisp clean white dresses, shaking their handkerchiefs at each other as they exchanged whispers. Three of the girls had curled their hair for the occasion and one had braided red ribbons through her tresses.

The hardwood floors were swept clean and the clear windows in the tiny church had been scrubbed until they shone. Even though it was built to hold only seventy-five people, the church was packed and folks were standing in the back to witness this special occasion.

Finally the side door opened and in walked the Reverend Dean George A. Beecher. Silence fell in the small building. The imposing man strode to the altar on his right. Turning to face the congregation, he smiled down at the eleven girls sitting before him and began the service.

Reverend Beecher was an Episcopal priest from Omaha. He was in Keystone on that Sunday, August 16, 1908, to deliver a special message and to dedicate the Little Church of Keystone.

Throughout the service, Reverend Beecher often referenced the young girls on the pew before him. He made it known to all who attended that it was because of those girls that the church had been built at all.

For several years, since the early part of the 1900s, those eleven girls, under the direction of Mrs. Georgia Paxton, had worked hard to raise funds and promote the building of a church for the residents of Keystone. Mrs. Paxton was the wife of a local rancher and she had organized the young girls into a service group called the King's Daughters. The girls, now teenagers, had spent much of their time together organizing bake sales, bazaars, and suppers, all in an attempt to raise money to buy materials to build a church.

Their efforts had yielded a sum just over three hundred dollars. Citizens of Keystone applauded their achievement and more than matched that figure, bringing the total to $714.50. The girls then contacted Ed Case of Red Oak, Iowa, who was known for his carpentry skills. They told him what they envisioned and Mr. Case said he would take the job, but that it would cost twelve hundred dollars.

Devastated, the girls turned to their mentor, Georgia Paxton. Knowing how hard they had worked, Georgia and her husband, Bill, donated the remaining five hundred dollars needed to the girls. The wood was shipped to Keystone from Omaha and construction began. The structure consisted of one room that only measured eighteen feet by forty feet. It was called the Little Church of Keystone.

A month after Reverend Beecher dedicated the little building, Bishop Richard Scannell and Father Woulf, both of the Catholic Archdiocese of Omaha, arrived in Keystone. The date was September 15, 1908. Once again, the Little Church was filled to the brim with mostly the same people. Scannell and Woulf came through the side door and turned to the altar on their left. Holding up a special piece of parchment embossed with an intricate seal, Scannell and Woulf dedicated the Little Church of Keystone.

Why did the Little Church of Keystone get dedicated twice, once by an Episcopalian and once by two Catholic priests?

It all started with the young girls known as the King's Daughters. The girls knew the importance of a faith-filled life, but Keystone did not have a church in which to worship. The girls in the service organization were of different denominations, and decided if they could raise enough money to build one church, they would all share it. The piece of parchment brought by the Catholic priests was a special dispensation by the pope to allow Catholics to worship in the same building as Protestants.

Ed Case of Red Oak, Iowa, knew he had a unique job to do in building the Little Church of Keystone. Not only did he build a Protestant altar for the south end of the structure but, in addition, he constructed a Catholic altar for the north end. He also made the pews with specially hinged backs so they could be moved to face whichever altar was in use at the time.

As the twentieth century rolled along, the town of Keystone grew smaller and smaller. Residents moved away, many to nearby Ogallala. The Presbyterians were the first to give up on the Little Church, with their final services taking place in 1926. Three years later, in 1929, the Catholics bid farewell. The Lutherans continued to use the church regularly until 1949. Today, the dual church is only used for special occasions, mostly weddings. And, even though the town of Keystone is unincorporated, the memories of those eleven girls and what they created linger on.

HE AIN'T HEAVY, HE'S M' BROTHER

1921

By the time the sun arose on October 22, 1921, the boys had already been up several hours, packing and cleaning. It was a crisp fall Saturday morning in Omaha, the kind of day when good things happened. That's what Eddie's mom used to say.

Eddie was one of the boys packing belongings into wheelbarrows and suitcases. He didn't think about his mom much anymore; the ache of her passing had lessened over the last year. But this morning, Eddie found his thoughts straying to her again and again. It was the anniversary of her death.

Eddie was one of more than one hundred boys who lived in Father Edward J. Flanagan's Home for Boys in downtown Omaha. Most who came were orphans, like Eddie, but some were wards of the court. There were some who had been in trouble with the law and some whose parents simply couldn't handle them anymore. Father Flanagan was sure that all boys were good souls deep down. He often said they just needed a little kindness and love in their lives.

Father Flanagan's Home for Boys had been open nearly four years now and hundreds of young boys had walked the halls. They slept dormitory-style in the larger rooms of the house and ate together in the dining rooms. The boys who stayed were required to attend church and some had even formed a baseball team, Eddie included.

When Eddie came to the Home for Boys after his mother died, Father Flanagan was the first person he met. At first, Eddie didn't want to talk to the imposing priest, but after a bit, Father Flanagan's Irish charm opened Eddie's heart and the story of his mother's short illness and death came rushing out. Eddie was embarrassed to find he was crying in front of this strange man, but Father Flanagan took it all in stride and welcomed Eddie into the home.

Today, Eddie was as excited as anybody for what was about to happen. He knew Father Flanagan, a man Eddie now adored and idolized, had been praying and planning for a long time to expand his Home for Boys. Father Flanagan had announced a few months ago that he found the perfect spot for new location. It was a 160-acre tract of land about ten miles west of Omaha called Overlook Farm. Today was moving day.

Eddie finished putting the last of the blankets into a rusty wheelbarrow and looked out the front windows onto the street below. Two large trucks blocked the street and pieces of furniture, including beds and tables, were being loaded into the backs of each. Dozens of boys were running around, trying to be helpful but mostly just getting in the way. Father Flanagan stood on the front steps, directing the flow of traffic.

Pushing the wheelbarrow in front of him, Eddie maneuvered it down the front stairs and out onto the lawn. Then he walked up to Father Flanagan.

Father Flanagan looked down at Eddie and smiled. "'Tis a great day for our Home for Boys, Eddie," he said. "When I started the home, I never imagined we'd be able to have such a fine place to live."

"What's it going to be like, Father?" asked Eddie.

"Ah, it's a grand farm," Father Flanagan said, sweeping his arms out to the side. "Acres of trees of all kinds next to acres of open fields. We'll be growing corn and alfalfa and beans and there is even an orchard!"

Eddie was impressed. He had never been out of Omaha and didn't know what life on a farm was going to be like. "Are we going to have to do chores?" he asked.

Father Flanagan laughed. "Yes, Eddie, we will. The farm has barns and sheds and a chicken coop, so we'll be plenty busy." Father Flanagan looked up at the loaded trucks and clapped his hands to get everyone's attention. The boys turned to face him, listening intently.

"We are ready to go to our new home," Father Flanagan said. His voice wasn't loud, but it carried to all parts of the yard. "We are leaving the city behind, the only home most of you have known. You will live in our new place full time and learn a trade. We will be a family." Father Flanagan smiled at the serious faces in front him. "The trucks are going to head west on Dodge Street and we'll follow on foot pushing these wheelbarrows and pulling the suitcases." He gestured to the wheelbarrows and suitcases littering the yard. "Grab what you can carry and let's go home."

Conversation started up again as the boys sorted out who would carry what. The trucks roared to life and started down the street. Father Flanagan took hold of a suitcase and followed the trucks, leading a straggling line of boys. Eddie grabbed another suitcase and ran to catch up with Father Flanagan.

"Father?" he asked. "What are we going to name our new home?"

Father Flanagan smiled down at Eddie as they headed west. "Well, my son, I think we'll call her 'Boys Town.'"

Father Flanagan's Boys Town grew quickly. The 160-acre farm soon was home to brick buildings used as dormitories, a chapel, classrooms, a dining hall, and offices. The boys learned woodworking, broom making, carpentry, baking, barbering, tailoring, printing, and agriculture. They also played organized sports such as baseball, basketball, boxing, and football. Boys Town was nicknamed the City of Little Men.

The citizens of Omaha supported Boys Town from the beginning. During the Great Depression of the 1930s, locals raised four hundred thousand dollars for a new trade school and gymnasium. In 1936, Boys Town was incorporated as a formal Nebraska village and received its own post office.

Nationwide interest in Boys Town grew after a 1938 movie of the same name was released. Starring Spencer Tracy and Mickey Rooney, the movie *Boys Town* was filmed partly on the property and featured many of the boys as extras. Tracy received the Best Actor Academy Award for his portrayal of Father Flanagan, increasing awareness of Boys Town. The film also won the Academy Award for Best Screenplay.

As the years rolled by, Boys Town continued to grow, as did the city around it. Once ten miles from town, Boys Town is now surrounded by suburban Omaha and is open to both boys and girls. More than five hundred youth live, work, and play at Boys Town today.

In the early 1900s, Father Edward J. Flanagan saw a need in downtown Omaha and filled it with his Home for Boys. Today, that ideal lives on throughout the world and is best illustrated by the Boys Town motto: "He ain't heavy, he's m' brother."

KOOL-AID, ANYONE?

1927

Edwin Perkins placed the open telegram on his desk and sighed. Leaning back in his chair, he took off his glasses and rubbed at his tired eyes.

Edwin's wife, Kitty, poked her head in the office.

"Bad news, dear?" she asked.

Edwin sat up and reached for the telegram. "Yes, bad news. The latest shipment of Fruit Smack is a total loss." Kitty gasped and rushed into the tiny office, reaching for the telegram. "Oh, no!" she cried. She scanned the telegram. "'All bottles broken . . . syrup everywhere . . . complete loss.' Oh, Edwin, I'm so sorry."

Kitty handed back the telegram and sat down across from Edwin. "What are you going to do?"

Edwin looked at Kitty fondly. He pictured her as a young girl, rushing into his father's general store with a new product she wanted them to carry. Her eyes were bright, and her smile was so wide. Edwin fell for her at that moment. She had been carrying a box of powdered mix called Jell-O.

Suddenly Edwin froze. Powdered mix. Could it be that simple? Could he take his popular Fruit Smack syrup and make it into a powdered mix and sell it that way? Why not? It had to work.

"Kitty, you're a genius," Edwin said, leaping to his feet. "I have to get to work right away." He dashed out the office without another word.

"Gee, thanks, I think," Kitty said to an empty office. She slowly got up and walked out of the office into the production area of the warehouse. It was 1927.

All of Edwin's life had been leading up to that moment in his warehouse. Born to David and Kizzie Perkins in Iowa in 1889, Edwin and his family moved to southern Nebraska in 1893. They lived in a sod house until 1900, when they moved to the small community of Hendley, Nebraska. Edwin's father opened D.M. Perkins General Merchandise store in Hendley.

Edwin worked for his father in the general store from the time he was eleven years old. One day after school, Edwin was stocking the shelves when Kitty Shoemaker walked in with a small cardboard box. She explained that she had recently been in Hastings, Nebraska, a large town about ninety miles northeast of Hendley, and had found the box for sale at a local grocery store. It was called Jell-O. The consumer only needed to add water to the powdered mix and they would have gelatin!

Edwin was fascinated, not only with Kitty, but also with the idea of mass marketing a food product such as Jell-O. He convinced his father to carry the powdered mix. The boxes sold for ten cents each.

Soon after, at age fourteen, Edwin sent away for a mail-order laboratory and began making concoctions in his mother's kitchen. He experimented with perfumes, lotions, and hair gels, in addition to other products. Edwin graduated high school in 1909 and went into business for himself. He purchased a printing press and published a weekly newspaper called the *Hendley Delphic*. He also worked as Hendley's postmaster from 1914 to 1918. During all this time, Edwin continued to experiment in his laboratory and even started his own direct mail enterprise named Perkins Products Company.

The year 1918 was a big one for Edwin. He and Kitty married and she joined him in his fledgling business. Their first success came in the form of a smoking cessation creation titled Nix-O-Tine Tobacco Remedy. Edwin invented a collection of chewable and powdered herbs, which, taken along with a special mouthwash and laxative, would cure any smoker. Edwin targeted returning World War I soldiers and Nix-O-Tine became the number one seller for the Perkins Products Company.

Edwin and Kitty moved the Perkins Products Company from Hendley to nearby Hastings in 1920 and expanded the direct mail business to include such products as perfume, shaving cream, spices, medicines, and lotions. In 1921, Edwin hit upon another winner in the form of a prepackaged drink called Fruit Smack.

Fruit Smack was the Perkins Products Company best seller from 1921 until 1927. It was sold as a bottled syrup in six flavors, with the customers adding sugar, water, and ice at home. Fruit Smack was not without its problems, however. The bottles tended to break during shipping and the contents sometimes spoiled.

Edwin had been inspired by Jell-O, which was manufactured and distributed by General Foods. For most of 1927, Edwin and his employees, all family members, worked hard at distilling the Fruit Smack syrup into powdered form. Finally, Edwin announced he had a new product to introduce to the market. It was a small package filled with one ounce of powder. When the customer added sugar and water, the powder became a fruity drink. Edwin named it Kool-Aid.

In 1927, the local grocery store in Hastings was the only place to purchase Kool-Aid. It came in raspberry, cherry, strawberry, grape, orange, and lemon-lime flavors. Each package cost ten cents and made ten glasses of Kool-Aid. The one-ounce packages were sold in special cartons meant to be displayed on countertops, right at the customer's fingertips. Orders began pouring in.

Within two years, Kool-Aid was sold across the United States. Edwin and his family continued working out of their downtown Hastings factory, using ice cream scoops to fill the paper packages and sealing them by hand. In 1929, Edwin hired Howard Lessard to be his chief chemist for Kool-Aid. Only Edwin and Howard knew the formula for the mix.

Kool-Aid became so popular that Edwin moved the factory to Chicago in 1931 to be closer to shipping lines. Many of his family employees came with him. All other items in the Perkins Products Company were discontinued—all 125 of them! The company now solely focused on Kool-Aid.

Since the beginning, Edwin had sold Kool-Aid at ten cents a package. With the Great Depression still going strong, Edwin wanted to give a boost to the economy, so he dropped the price to five cents a package. Sales did not suffer one bit and the price stayed at five cents for the next thirty years.

What started as a boy mixing up concoctions for fun transformed to a small, family-run mail order company. That evolved into a multimillion-dollar industry and made Edwin Perkins famous. By the time Edwin was ready to retire in 1953, none other than General Foods, the company he had so admired for their distribution of Jell-O, came knocking to buy the rights to Kool-Aid.

Today, Kool-Aid can be found at nearly every grocery store and food sales facility in North America. Perkins' six original flavors have expanded to more than twenty and Kool-Aid has become a household name. Not bad for a Nebraska boy messing around in his mother's kitchen.

A HELPING HEART

1936

The letter came with the morning mail. David Kaufmann had spent a productive morning on the floor of his dime store, showing a new employee the stocking procedures. He worked an hour behind the soda counter and another hour working on advertising. Things were going well for David Kaufmann in his Grand Island store.

The letter was from his cousin, Feo. Feo and her husband, Isidor Kahn, lived in Germany, Kaufmann's home country. Kaufmann, who had emigrated to the United States in 1903 when he was twenty-seven years old, had been back to Germany for a visit several years before and had told Feo that if she ever wanted to come to America, he would help get her settled. It was now 1936 and Feo was asking for Cousin David's help.

Kaufmann frowned as he squinted at the letter. He knew of Adolf Hitler's rise to power in Germany, but hadn't heard how tensions had escalated between Hitler's supporters and Jews living in Germany. Feo's letter spoke of anti-Semitic remarks yelled at her on the street, about a rock thrown through their window, about how frightened they were becoming of going out of their house at all.

Family was important to David Kaufmann, so he did what he thought was right. He contacted the immigration office and declared his intent to bring Feo and Isi to America. Kaufmann was given an affidavit of support to fill out and detailed Feo and Isi's names, gender, ages, places of birth, and relationship with him. He also had to swear Feo and Isi both were in good health and physical condition. In signing the affidavit, Kaufmann had to vow he would be responsible for them and their welfare and that they would not be a burden to the United States. He swore he was a law-abiding citizen with financial stability. Both were true statements about David Kaufmann; after emigrating to the United States, Kaufmann had applied for citizenship, even as he opened his own five-and-dime store in Grand Island. The store opened in 1906 and Kaufmann became a US citizen in 1910.

Kaufmann didn't speak any English when he first came to the United States, but soon taught himself the language. In Germany he had worked in sales and retail and he continued that career in America. Kaufmann's store in Grand Island was a commercial success and Kaufmann himself found personal happiness in 1924, when, at the age of forty-nine, he married one of his employees, Celia.

There were over a dozen Jewish families in Grand Island in the beginning of the twentieth century and even though there wasn't a synagogue, those families were able to get together for Jewish high holy days and social activities. Kaufmann was involved in these and was able to perform rites in the ceremonies.

When he received the letter from his cousin Feo, Kaufmann was worried about his Jewish family and their fate in Germany. He wanted to do what he could, so after he signed an affidavit of support, he also sent a fifty-dollar personal check to Feo and Isi. They wanted to escape from Nazi Germany, and David Kaufmann made that happen.

When Feo and Isi arrived in the United States, they quickly made their way to Grand Island. Isi found a job at Kaufmann's store. This could be the end of the story, but there is more. Feo fretted about those family members they left behind. She approached Kaufmann to discuss bringing more family over to the United States.

By all accounts, David Kaufmann was a kind man. But it was more than kindness that prompted Kaufmann to spend the next decade signing affidavit after affidavit in support of family members he didn't even remember, all in an effort to get them out of Nazi Germany. By the end of World War II, fifty-seven thousand German Jews had emigrated to the United States; David Kaufmann was responsible for hundreds of them. He personally signed for nearly ninety families, most of whom were distant cousins or cousins of cousins. To each family he sent a fifty-dollar personal check. That amount in today's currency would be about one thousand dollars. A few of those families came to Grand Island, but most settled in other parts of the country. Some of those family members achieved citizenship and in turn signed affidavits of support for many others.

Even as Kaufmann was saving lives with the stroke of his pen, life went on in Nebraska. Kaufmann's store continued to do well and he received Grand Island's Distinguished Citizen Award in 1935. His wife, Celia, passed away in 1942, and in 1945 he married his second wife, Madeline. In October of 1955, on Kaufmann's eightieth birthday, his family, including all those distant cousins he helped bring to America, surprised Kaufmann with arranging to have 170 trees planted in Israel in honor of his generosity. Kaufmann died in 1969 at age ninety-three.

There are men like David Kaufmann all over America. They are hard working and intelligent. They are kind and compassionate. They are giving and honest. David Kaufmann was a hero to the hundreds of Jews he helped escape Nazi Germany, but no one knew it. He did not publicize his deeds or seek accolades or recognition. He simply did what he knew was right and saved lives in the process.

HERE'S JOHNNY

1937

Johnny pedaled as hard as he could. He zoomed down the quiet residential street, his bike swerving to avoid cars and pedestrians alike. The twelve-year-old didn't spare a glance at the traffic. He was a boy on a mission.

For the past three days, Johnny had raced home from school in the northeast Nebraska community of Norfolk in time to greet the mailman who came to his door. Johnny had sent away to Chicago for a mail order magic kit and it was supposed to arrive any day now. He could barely contain his excitement over the thought of the magic kit.

The year was 1937. Johnny and his family had been living in Norfolk for four years and they were settled in. Johnny's dad, Homer, worked for the local public power district and, even though times were hard throughout the Midwest, had saved enough money to buy Johnny a bike a few years previously.

Johnny was born on October 23, 1925, in Corning, Iowa. He and his family, including older sister Catherine and younger brother Dick, moved around southwest Iowa for many years, following Homer's work. Now the family lived in a modest bungalow close to downtown Norfolk.

Johnny steered his bicycle into his front yard and raced up the wooden steps to the porch. He spied the mailman walking away from his house. The mail had already come today! On the porch, Johnny's mother, Ruth, was waiting for him, a wrapped parcel in her hands.

"It came today," she said.

Johnny whooped with joy and snatched the parcel from his mother's grip. Tearing off the wrapping, he gazed in wonder at the magic kit for which he had waited so long. The kit promised to make him a star with tricks such as the Amazing Dancing Cane and the Interlocking Rings. Johnny looked up at his mom, a grin splitting his boyish face.

Johnny Carson, entertainer, had arrived.

For the next several years, Johnny Carson practiced his magic every chance he could get. He billed himself as "The Great Carsoni" and wore a hand-sewn cape for his appearances. He performed for classmates and church groups, and was even paid three dollars for his talents by the local Kiwanis Club. Carson's parents supported his need to entertain and encouraged him to continue, even as he worked to graduate high school.

In school, Carson was not an athlete, but was involved in music, drama, and journalism. He also held down a part-time job as an usher at the local movie theater. Through it all, he continued to practice his magic act.

After graduation, Carson, like so many young men of his generation, enlisted in the Navy. Before he left for training, however, Carson took a quick vacation, hitchhiking his way to California. He liked what he saw in Hollywood and decided to come back after his time in the Navy was over.

As World War II raged on, Carson went through the Naval officer training program. At age twenty he was on his way to action in the Pacific Ocean aboard the USS *Pennsylvania*. However, before he could see any battles, the war ended. Even though Carson served as a communications officer, decoding encrypted messages, he spent much of his time entertaining his fellow sailors with his magic.

Carson's dreams of Hollywood were put on hold after he was honorably discharged from the service in 1946. At his parents' urging, he enrolled in the University of Nebraska in Lincoln, studying speech and drama. Carson worked hard during his college years, both in the classroom and out of it. Carson was a member of the Phi Gamma Delta fraternity and worked part time at the local radio station KFAB. He graduated college in just three years after presenting a thesis titled, "How to Write Comedy Jokes."

Carson's work in college at KFAB led to a job at the prominent Omaha radio station WOW in 1950. WOW had introduced a television channel the previous year, and it wasn't long before Carson was writing comedy sketches and announcing commercials on both the radio and television sides of the station.

Soon Carson was hosting his own television show on WOW called *The Squirrel's Nest.* Carson would intersperse comedy with thoughts on daily life in the Midwest. That down-home humor became the basis for Carson's comedy style for the rest of his life.

Johnny Carson left Nebraska for good in 1951, moving to Los Angeles to become a staff announcer for a radio station. He worked his way around Hollywood and soon became a writer for famed comedian Red Skelton. Carson's big break came one night when Skelton was injured during a rehearsal and Johnny was asked to fill in. Carson opened the show with a simple, self-effacing monologue. He was a hit.

Carson continued to search for fame, moving to New York City in 1955. He bounced around from show to show, gaining popularity and experience. Finally, in 1962, twenty-five years after receiving his mail order magic kit, Carson was given the job of a lifetime as the host of the popular *Tonight Show.* Carson would shine in that job for the next thirty years, becoming one of the most respected and admired comedians in Hollywood. Johnny Carson retired in 1992 and passed away in 2005. He remains one of Nebraska's favored sons.

SHARPIE

1938

Sharpie smiled for the camera as she leaned against her plane. The photographer took one last shot and indicated he was finished. Sharpie straightened up and looked at the crowd gathered on the field.

This was a historic day for Evelyn Sharp, and for the state of Nebraska. It was May 19, 1938, and Evelyn, or "Sharpie," as she was known, was about to become the nation's first female airmail pilot.

Sharpie had grown up with a love of the sky in her blood. Born in Montana in 1919, Sharpie was adopted by John and Mary Sharp, who moved their small family to Nebraska a few years later. In 1930, when Sharpie was eleven years old, their family settled in Ord, Nebraska.

As a girl, Sharpie worked for her dad, selling ice-cream cones out of a handmade cart. Their horse was hitched to the front and pulled the cart through town. Sharpie walked along beside the cart, hawking her wares. Even though she suffered from severe asthma, Sharpie learned to love all things athletic, including dancing, horseback riding, tennis, and swimming. She was extremely involved in various school activities, like band and choir, and the Campfire Girls organization.

But flying was Sharpie's main love. At age fifteen, she began taking flying lessons from Jack Jefford of Jefford's Aviation Services in Broken Bow, Nebraska. Jefford was staying with her family and, in lieu of paying room and board, he offered to give Sharpie flying lessons.

Sharpie convinced her parents to accept Jefford's proposal and she soon took to the skies. Her first time in the air was February 3, 1935, and thirteen months later, Sharpie completed her first solo flight.

Sharpie's training included takeoffs and landings and learning loops and figure-eights. Due to Nebraska's climate and terrain, she also learned to land her plane on such unique surfaces as a cornfield and the frozen North Loop River.

Just over a year after she started her lessons, Sharpie earned her amateur pilot's license in June 1936. She was just sixteen.

One year later, Evelyn Sharp graduated from high school named as the Best Girl Athlete. She continued to pursue her love of flying, even as she kept busy teaching swimming lessons and lifesaving that summer. But the end of summer would bring a big surprise for the budding aviatrix.

In August 1937, just a few months after she graduated from high school, a group of Ord businessmen invited Sharpie to join them at the airfield for a special presentation. The businessmen had purchased a new plane just for Sharpie.

Sharpie was amazed and overwhelmed. She wanted to earn her living as a pilot and vowed to pay back the community of Ord for their generosity. Sharpie knew she needed to earn her transport license in order to charge passengers for flights or to accept a job as a pilot. Earning her transport license became her number one goal.

Before she could do that, Sharpie had to also earn a commercial pilot's license. She did that the following year and, at age eighteen, became the youngest licensed woman pilot in Nebraska and only one of just over four hundred in the United States. Sharpie earned her commercial license by meticulously tracking her flight hours. She spent much of her air time doing promotional work for the businessmen of Ord who had purchased her first plane for her.

When her first attempt on earning the transport license failed, Sharpie knew she had to make a change. She moved to Lincoln and spent a few months attending a flight school. The move paid off; on May 13, 1938, Sharpie achieved her goal and was awarded a transport license. At the time, Sharpie was the only completely commercially licensed female pilot in the entire state.

Sharpie's first job as a commercial transport pilot came six days later, when she was hired to deliver airmail in rural Nebraska. Hundreds of well-wishers turned out to greet Sharpie in the towns of Ord, Greeley, and Grand Island. With her first run that morning, Evelyn Sharp officially became the nation's first female airmail pilot. Sharpie delivered twenty-five hundred pieces of mail that first day, and much of it was fan mail addressed to her!

Now that she had her commercial transport license and was working delivering airmail, Sharpie began the long process of paying off the Ord businessmen who had been so generous to her a few years previous. She continued to advertise for the businesses with her plane and began "barnstorming," or taking paying customers for rides in her plane.

But rural Nebraska was not enough for Sharpie. Taking the next challenge, Sharpie passed her flight instructor rerating test in June of 1940 and could now teach flying to others. Her first job was teaching 350 men how to fly at the Civilian Pilot Training Program in Spearfish, South Dakota. Sharpie was only twenty years old.

Within a year, Sharpie moved to California. She continued to teach flying and worked in movies for a bit. She lived with other female pilots from around the United States and talk often turned to the inequities faced by female pilots in a male-dominated industry.

The advent of World War II only heightened Sharpie's frustrations. She and her female colleagues were unable to join the service as pilots, even though they were entirely qualified. In September of 1942, the Secretary of War finally formed the Women's Auxiliary Ferrying Squadron, a unit designed to ferry trainers and light aircraft from factories to military bases throughout the United States. Sharpie immediately signed up and, due to her qualifications, was admitted in October of 1942. The WAFS never numbered more than thirty women at a time and soon moved from ferrying trainers and light aircraft to actually flying bombers and heavy fighters from base to base.

Sharpie used this opportunity to see more of the United States. She could fly coast to coast in a day. Flying these unique aircraft for the US military was also a dream come true for Sharpie. She was learning about different types of aircraft and serving her country.

Sharpie's service was tragically cut short. On April 3, 1944, just eighteen months after joining the WAFS Squadron, the fighter she was piloting crashed in a field in Pennsylvania. Sharpie was thrown from the cockpit and died immediately. Evelyn Sharp was twenty-four.

During her whole life, Sharpie only wanted to fly. From the wide-open spaces of rural Nebraska to the rough mountains of California to the wooded hills of Pennsylvania, Sharpie used her intelligence and perseverance to achieve her dreams.

NORTH PLATTE CANTEEN

1941

Rae Wilson shifted her weight from one foot to the other in an effort to keep warm. The December wind howled around the deserted train depot and curled between Rae's legs as she waited. She shivered and huddled into her coat even more.

It was a clear, crisp December morning in 1941. Rae and several community members in North Platte, Nebraska, had gathered at the train depot to meet a special train scheduled to arrive any minute. Word had gotten out that North Platte's own Company D of the Nebraska National Guard would be on that train and the townspeople wanted to see their family and friends, even if it was just going to be for a short time.

Company D was one of hundreds of units mobilized in the wake of the attack on Pearl Harbor just a few days prior. The company was traveling from Camp Robinson, Arkansas, to the West Coast and would stop briefly at North Platte along the way. Rae and her friends had spent the past two days baking goodies and gathering gifts to distribute to the men when they stopped.

A whistle sounded in the distance. Rae craned her neck and saw the light of the engine coming down the track. Excitement mounted as the train pulled into the station. Rae searched the faces in the windows of the train for a familiar one belonging to her brother, a member of Company D. Rae's smile faded. Where was he? She couldn't spot him. In fact, none of these boys looked familiar.

One of the military personnel stepped off the train and approached the group. Rae stepped forward and introduced herself, still clutching her basket of goodies. Then she stopped, looked hard again at the faces in the window, and blurted out, "Who are you?"

The soldier laughed. "Why, we're from Company D," he said.

"But none of you look familiar," Rae replied, still confused.

"I don't know why we would," the soldier responded. "We're from Company D of the Kansas National Guard."

A small moan went through the crowd. Tensions had been running high since the Pearl Harbor attack and all the townsfolk knew the United States was going to war. They had hoped to get one last look at their loved ones before they left for service in the Pacific or elsewhere. Now, due to miscommunication, they were greeting the men from the Kansas National Guard, not the Nebraska National Guard.

Disappointment clearly showing on her face, Rae looked down helplessly at the basket in her hands.

"Well, this was to be for my brother, but I guess you can have it," she said slowly, handing the basket to the soldier in front of her.

With a look of confusion, the soldier took the basket from Rae and opened it. A smile split his face when he smelled the fresh cookies and cakes. He looked up at Rae.

"Really, ma'am?" he asked. "You are giving this to me?"

Rae found his smile was infectious. She grinned back. "Sure."

"Thank you!" the soldier said enthusiastically. "Thank you so much!"

Rae gestured to the other folks on the platform and they all approached the train. Soldiers were lowering the windows and hanging out the side of the train. One by one, the baskets of goodies were passed inside the train as shouts of "Thanks!" "Gee!" and "This is neat!" echoed up and down the tracks.

Soon the whistle blew again and the train started up. As it slowly made its way down the tracks, the soldiers leaned out the windows and waved, grinning ear to ear.

Rae and townspeople on the platform waved back until the train was out of sight. Then they turned and looked at each other. Even though they hadn't seen their own soldiers, they all felt uplifted by the visit. A plan began to form in Rae's mind.

For the next week, Rae solicited donations from North Platte businesses and organizations. The aim was clear. Rae wanted to open a canteen at the old Union Pacific passenger train depot to serve food, desserts, and other goods to soldiers on their way to the West Coast. The Red Cross had run a similar canteen at the depot during World War I, serving more than 113,000 soldiers in a seventeen-month period. Already there were several trains a day that made a ten-minute stop in North Platte. Rae recalled the smile of the soldier to whom she had given her basket that first day and knew this project would be a big morale booster for the soldiers.

Others in North Platte agreed. The outpouring of support was immense and by Christmas Day, 1941, the North Platte Canteen was ready to go.

The first trains came through before dawn and they continued throughout the day. At first, because troop movements were secret, a special code was used to gather volunteers to the depot. A calling tree was established with the phrase, "I have the coffee on," used to alert the volunteers that a train was coming.

As the days continued, the canteen grew in popularity and need. Each day, between three thousand and five thousand soldiers were supplied with coffee, treats, and magazines as they made the quick stop in North Platte. The volunteer base grew to include civic and service organizations and religious groups. After school, high school girls above the age of sixteen were employed as Platform Girls, greeting the train and directing the soldiers into the depot. Oftentimes, if the stop was an extra quick one and the soldiers did not have time to disembark, the Platform Girls distributed baskets of fruit and candy to the soldiers through the windows of the train.

Rae Wilson moved away from North Platte in 1942 and the North Platte Canteen fell under the leadership of Helen Christ, the wife of a Union Pacific conductor. Christ received the full support of Union Pacific, which supplied the canteen with heat, water, cups, napkins, a new dishwashing machine, and even hired a janitor for them.

As the popularity of the North Platte Canteen grew, so did the donations. The entire project was run on cash donations from local and area businesses at first, but those cash donations soon were rolling in from throughout the United States. Even President Franklin D. Roosevelt sent five dollars to the canteen to support its efforts.

In addition to food and snacks, the North Platte Canteen also supplied current magazines, toiletries, puzzles, and games to the soldiers. Any serviceman with a birthday was presented with a cake, and on Thanksgiving, soldiers were treated to a holiday meal complete with turkey, stuffing, and mashed potatoes.

The North Platte Canteen operated daily from Christmas Day, 1941, to April 1, 1946, some eight months after the war ended. During those last few months, the canteen served as a "Welcome Home" station for soldiers, still serving food, goods, and a smile.

In all, more than six million servicemen were served at the North Platte Canteen during its four-year run. The canteen was given the United States Meritorious Wartime Service Award for supplying more than goods to those servicemen. The volunteers at the North Platte Canteen also shared hope with a nation at war.

PROVING HIS LOYALTY

1941

—

When the Japanese bombed Pearl Harbor on the morning of December 7, 1941, life changed for every American. The actions of the Japanese catapulted the United States into World War II. Young men from all over the country rushed to their local recruiting offices to join the armed forces, eager to fight for their country.

Pearl Harbor changed everything for Ben and his brother, Fred, of Hershey, Nebraska. Ben was deeply disturbed by the actions of the Japanese and wanted to prove his loyalty to the United States by enlisting in the Army. On Monday, December 8, 1941, the day after the attack on Pearl Harbor, Ben and Fred headed to the recruiter's office in North Platte and put their names down for consideration. Then Ben and Fred stood in line with dozens of other young men, waiting for their names to be called to join the service.

They waited all day. Their names were never called.

Ben and Fred went home, expecting a phone call from the recruiter's office at any moment.

They waited nearly two weeks, but no call came.

Finally, Ben heard on the radio that the recruiter's office in Grand Island, Nebraska, was accepting all eligible young men. Ben called the Grand Island office and asked one question of the recruiter.

"Does race matter?"

The recruiter in Grand Island laughed and said, "I get paid two dollars a head, so I don't care what race you are! I'll sign you up fast."

Ben and Fred drove to Grand Island the next day and enlisted in the Army Air Corps. They soon shipped out to different bases, ready to serve their country. They wanted to get over their guilt about Pearl Harbor and the shame they felt.

You see, Ben and Fred Kuroki were Japanese.

◆──◆

In the early 1900s, Ben Kuroki's father emigrated from Japan to California and found work on the railroad. His job brought him to Nebraska. He loved it and decided to stay, sending for his wife to join him. Ben's father became a farmer and raised his American-born children on a farm near Hershey.

Ben and Fred had a typical American upbringing. They, along with their three other brothers and five sisters, worked the land with their parents, raising crops and vegetables. In their free time, Ben and his brothers would explore the North Platte River, hunting and fishing along its banks.

Ben graduated high school in 1936 as vice president of his senior class. After graduation, he bought a truck to help with the family's farm business, transporting vegetables to sell throughout the Midwest. He also took flying lessons in his free time and in the fall of 1941 completed his first solo flight.

As American-born children of Japanese ancestry, Ben, Fred, and the rest of the Kuroki children were known as Nisei. After the attack on Pearl Harbor, nationwide attitudes towards Nisei were strained. In February 1942, just two months after Pearl Harbor, President Franklin D. Roosevelt authorized sending 120,000 Japanese Americans to "war relocation camps" across the United States. Most camps were erected in the middle of the country, away from large cities. The

Nisei in Nebraska, including Ben's parents, remained free, but their movements were monitored and their bank accounts frozen.

Ben and Fred were both given menial jobs in the Army Air Corps, digging ditches and peeling potatoes. Ben was afraid to go near the big planes at his base, thinking someone would assume he was trying to sabotage them.

Ben was sent to England in the fall of 1942 with the 93rd bomb unit. He was working as a clerk for the unit, but in his spare time he would disassemble and reassemble different guns while blindfolded. His dream was to become a gunner in a B-24, known as a Liberator. Those planes were used in nearly all combat missions in Europe.

Ben's patriotism impressed his fellow soldiers. When a gunner position opened up, the commanding officer asked the other men if they would feel comfortable with Ben in that job. They agreed unanimously and Ben, nicknamed "Most Honorable Son," had a new assignment.

Ben's unit moved from England to Algeria, fighting German forces in Africa. Over the next fifteen months, Ben would fly in thirty missions, five more than what was recognized as a complete tour of duty. Those missions took him all over northern Africa and eastern Europe. His actions earned Ben a Distinguished Flying Cross medal from the Army Air Corps. He volunteered for the extra five missions in honor of his brother, Fred, who was still serving stateside.

After Ben's time in Europe, he came back to the United States and was stationed near Santa Monica, California. It was during this time that Ben became increasingly aware of the tensions between Americans and the Nisei. All of the Nisei living on the West Coast had been interned in camps and Ben drew curious stares from other citizens as he walked around in his highly decorated uniform.

The Army Air Corps had a new assignment for Ben; they wanted to use him as a publicity stunt to illustrate how smooth relations between Americans and Nisei could be. However, many places refused Ben service because of his race. He was scorned on the streets of America by his fellow citizens.

Ben was then sent to visit the Japanese Americans interned in the war relocation camps. While some welcomed him as a hero, many thought he was a traitor to their race and despised him.

Ben didn't like being a poster boy for the Army and wanted to get back into fighting. This time, he asked to be sent to the Pacific Theater to fly B-29s, the biggest of the bombers. It took several months for Ben's request to be accepted and even then there were many in the US government who didn't trust Ben and didn't want him anywhere near the bombers going to Japan.

But Ben prevailed and became the first Japanese-American soldier to fly combat missions in the Pacific. He flew more than twenty missions until the end of the war in 1945. The most serious injuries Ben sustained in his time in the Army Air Corps happened during the summer of 1945 when Ben and another soldier, a Native American, got into a fight over who was more patriotic. Ben was in the base hospital recovering from his wounds when he learned about the bombing of Hiroshima and the end of the war.

With a total of fifty-eight combat missions in both Europe and the Pacific under his belt, and three Distinguished Flying Crosses decorating his chest, Ben Kuroki came home a hero. He used the GI Bill to pay for school at the University of Nebraska and went on to become a newspaper editor. Ben's parents became naturalized citizens of the United States.

When Ben Kuroki thinks about his time in the armed forces, he knows how lucky he is to be alive. He also knows he had a tougher time than many other veterans. His own words illustrate that point: "I had to fight like hell for the right to fight for my own country," he has said. From a feeling of shame after the bombing of Pearl Harbor to taking pride in his country, Ben Kuroki is a true American hero.

POW IN THE PLAINS

1943

The year was 1943. War was raging in Europe and in the Pacific. American soldiers were shipped by the thousands to the front lines, leaving behind a shortage of workers in the factories and farms of the United States.

In many cities, those jobs were filled by wives, sisters, and even mothers of soldiers far away. However, in a few areas of the country, the government chose to send prisoners of war, or POWs, to work for the good of America.

William Oberdieck was one of those prisoners. Born in 1922 in Mulheim, Germany, Oberdieck majored in business and languages and was drafted into the German army in 1941. Because of his college background, Oberdieck worked intelligence with the German Afrika Korps in northern Africa.

The war was not going well for the Germans in Africa. The weather was hot and dusty and the soldiers were rationed one cup of water per day. Oberdieck knew his unit was about to be captured, so one night he slipped away from camp under the cover of darkness and began working his way westward across north Africa, hoping to reach Spain and then work his way home to Germany. His ability to speak German, English, French, Spanish, and Italian served him well and he evaded capture for many weeks.

Oberdieck was eventually caught and found out to be a German soldier. After more than a month at a POW camp in Scotland, he was placed on a ship and sent to the United States.

There were more than five hundred POW camps throughout the Midwest, including just over twenty in Nebraska. Oberdieck was sent to a camp in Kansas first, but soon found himself relocating to Camp Atlanta near Holdrege, Nebraska. Oberdieck would spend most of the next three years in Camp Atlanta while the war continued.

Oberdieck was one of three thousand POWs interned at Camp Atlanta from 1943 until the end of the war in 1945. The camp had its own train stop so prisoners could be loaded and unloaded from the train without danger to the local population. The camp also boasted a chapel, hospital, bakery, laundry, and PX, a store where soldiers could purchase food, candy, books, beer, and jewelry.

The prisoners found the POW camps clean and comfortable. While the citizens of Atlanta, Nebraska, were nervous at first about supposedly dangerous enemy soldiers living so close to them, the prisoners and local folks got along. In fact, due to the steady influx of immigrants to the United States in the years preceding the war, many prisoners actually had family in the area who were allowed to visit on a regular basis.

The POWs were allowed to work outside the camp for farmers and local factories. They were even paid for their work. Oberdieck spent his years at Camp Atlanta working at a chicken processing plant in Alma, Nebraska, and also helped with potato and tomato harvests, vaccinating hogs, and quarrying rocks.

Oberdieck spent some of his time at a POW camp in Weeping Water, about two hundred miles east of Camp Atlanta. It was during this time that Oberdieck found his life's work, although he didn't know it at the time. Some of the POWs were assigned to travel from Weeping Water to Nebraska City during the fall harvest season to work at a local apple orchard. The owners of the orchard, Richard and Laurine Kimmel, accepted the help of the German prisoners readily and developed a friendship with Oberdieck. At Kimmel Orchard, Oberdieck learned how to care for apples and run an orchard.

In May 1945, Germany surrendered to Allied Forces. Three months later, in August of that year, Japan also surrendered. The war was over. For the 425,000 Germans and Italians being held in POW camps in the United States, this meant their time of incarceration was over. By October of 1945, most of the POW camps in Nebraska, including those in Atlanta and Weeping Water, were closed.

Oberdieck was sent back to Europe and his family. Although he was happy to be home and out of the war, Oberdieck never forgot the kindness he was shown while he was a prisoner in Nebraska. After marrying and starting a family in his home country of Germany, Oberdieck decided to make a new home. He traveled with his young family back to Nebraska.

Oberdieck was hired by Richard and Laurine Kimmel to continue his previous job at their orchard. He settled his family in Nebraska City and in 1964, purchased Kimmel Orchard from Richard and Laurine. Oberdieck ran the orchard until his retirement in 1990.

The words "prisoner of war camp" do not always bring up a positive picture, but for William Oberdieck, being a POW in the plains changed his life for the better.

AN IMPORTANT BOMBER

1945

It was June 1945. The assembly line at Fort Crook in Bellevue was busy as usual. For the past five years, since before the United States' involvement in World War II, bombers had been built at Fort Crook, mostly B-26s and B-29s, and it seemed they were rolling out faster than ever.

One B-29 Superfortress bomber in particular would have garnered special attention that day, if the workers could see the future. This specific B-29 would be named after the mother of the pilot who would fly her for a secret mission over Japan. That bomber, named *Enola Gay,* would carry the first atomic bomb to be dropped on Hiroshima, Japan, in August of that year.

No one working in the 1.2-million-square-foot bomber plant that hot summer day could foresee the end of the war just two months later. Certainly no one anticipated the future prominence of Fort Crook, which had served in a variety of capacities since it was established in the 1890s.

Fort Crook was created in Bellevue, Nebraska's oldest community, between Omaha to the north and the Platte River to the south. The town began as a fur trading post in the early 1800s and was incorporated in 1855, one year after Nebraska became an official US territory. Before Fort Crook was established, Bellevue was declining in population and popularity, having lost both the bid for the capital and the railroad to Omaha (the capital later moved to Lincoln). Fort Crook originally was needed to provide additional military facilities to those stationed at Fort Omaha just to the north. It was used as training grounds and as a recuperation center until after World War I. In 1921, an airfield was added, although that event was not without controversy. After the field was completed, it was discovered that a nearby large oak tree was in the way of planes landing and taking off from the field. A few servicemen took matters into their own hands and, late one night, strategically placed sticks of dynamite around the tree. There wasn't much of the tree left by morning. The controversy arose about a month later when officials from the Nebraska Historical Society visited Fort Crook and wanted to know what happened to the oldest tree in the county.

Tree or no tree, the strip was named Offutt Field after Lieutenant Jarvis J. Offutt, the first Omahan killed during World War I. For the next several years, Fort Crook and Offutt Field became the base for the US Post Office airmail service and hosted a US Weather Bureau station.

In January 1948, the newly created US Air Force renamed Fort Crook as Offutt Air Force Base. Later that same year, General Curtis E. LeMay, commander of the Strategic Air Command (SAC) in Maryland, declared his intention to move SAC away from the East Coast. LeMay believed the coastal areas were too easy to reach by enemies of the United States and was concerned with the lack of physical space surrounding the current headquarters, Andrews Air

Force Base. LeMay searched through the nation's list of new Air Force bases and zeroed in on Offutt.

One big draw Offutt Air Force Base had to LeMay was its runway. The field, now twenty-seven years old and definitely treeless, was one of the only runways in the nation that could handle the landing and takeoff of fully loaded B-29 bombers. Offutt Air Force Base could serve as the headquarters for SAC immediately.

As the United States entered the Cold War in the 1950s, the importance of SAC and Offutt Air Force Base was fully realized. The staff at SAC was focused on nuclear threat from the Soviet Union and created a vast underground combat operations center from which they could watch and respond to potential missile attacks. Every piece of military intelligence was filtered through this mid-sized base located in a mid-sized town in the middle of the Midwest.

The economic effect Offutt Air Force Base has had on the state of Nebraska is incalculable. Hundreds of thousands of armed forces personnel have served their time at Offutt, spending their money in Bellevue and Omaha, completing their education at the University of Nebraska Omaha or Creighton University. Many civilian jobs have been created to serve Offutt Air Force Base as well.

As the Cold War waned in the 1990s, SAC was dissolved. Nuclear reduction treaties called for the limiting of nuclear weapons and the limiting of personnel. Offutt Air Force Base continues to be a vital force in the United States military; it is now home to STRATCOM, the US Strategic Command, under the Department of Defense. STRATCOM does much the same as SAC, providing surveillance and reconnaissance to the US Armed Forces.

On that summer day in 1945, the workers at Fort Crook's Building D were doing more than assembling bombers. They were building a future military stronghold.

CENTER PIVOT IRRIGATION

1947

Frank Zybach liked to tinker. The Colorado farmer had grown up in the early 1900s near Columbus, Nebraska, and was often found helping his blacksmith father with work or chores around the farm. Although Zybach was twenty-six years old before he applied for his first official patent, he had been creating tools and equipment to help make farming life easier since he was a teenager.

Zybach enjoyed tinkering more than he enjoyed farming, but none of his inventions had ever made it big. It was now 1947 and Zybach, who had not attended school past the seventh grade, was in his fifties and farming in Colorado. One day, Zybach watched workers at a neighboring farm struggle to move heavy and awkward tubes of water from one row to another to irrigate the fields. Zybach knew there had to be an easier way of irrigating cropland.

Zybach went home and started doing what he did best, tinkering. He knew the most common ways to irrigate land included digging a furrow between rows of crops and flooding it with water, collecting rainfall, utilizing underground wells, and, most commonly, the technique of drip irrigation, where laborers would move pipes and tubes of water from row to row, letting water drip out of the tubes for a certain amount of time before moving them again. Drip irrigation was the most effective, but also very costly, both in manpower and time.

Zybach dreamed of creating a water-propelled irrigation system on wheels. If he could attach the base of the contraption to a well head and move water through the pipes to evenly spaced sprinklers, the water would propel the system around the field in a circular motion. Guide wires attached to the contraption would help even out the pace of the machine.

Using the tools and materials he had on hand, and making from scratch things he needed but didn't have, Zybach created such a machine. It was the first center pivot irrigation system in the world.

Zybach's creation worked like he had hoped. In 1949, he applied for a patent for the "Zybach Self-Propelled Sprinkler Apparatus." In 1952, the patent was his and Zybach continued to tinker with the new irrigation system, making changes and corrections to the design to improve it. Once he had his patent, Zybach moved back to Nebraska to manufacture the new farming equipment and take advantage of the Ogallala Aquifer.

The Ogallala Aquifer is the largest collection of groundwater in the world, covering 174,000 square miles in the central plains. The aquifer spreads under nearly the entire state of Nebraska and provides nearly two million people with drinking water in Nebraska, north into South Dakota, west into Wyoming, Colorado, and New Mexico, and south into Kansas, Oklahoma, and Texas. Zybach's invention brought more water to the surface of Nebraska, helping farmers irrigate their crops more efficiently.

Zybach's invention happened at just the right time for success to occur. Even as far back as the late 1800s, settlers in Nebraska and the central plains knew there was water to be had under the ground.

Improved well-digging technology and the invention of center pivot irrigation collided in Nebraska in the mid-twentieth century directly above the Ogallala Aquifer.

However, moving his invention to Nebraska brought Zybach face to face with another problem. The tall corn of Nebraska couldn't fit under the low pipes of Zybach's apparatus. Zybach had built it with the low crops of eastern Colorado, like sugar beets and alfalfa, in mind. Zybach raised the pipes and started manufacturing irrigation machines in his backyard.

By 1954, Zybach realized he needed help with his invention. He sold his patent to the Valley Manufacturing Company in Valley, Nebraska, a small community just southeast of Fremont. Valley Manufacturing Company expanded upon Zybach's design, perfecting the technique and design, and added a feature that allowed fertilizer to be pumped through the pipes along with the water.

Zybach's invention revolutionized farming in America and around the world. Using a center pivot design and allowing the water to propel the machine evenly distributed the water and cut down on labor costs. Valley Manufacturing, which became Valmont Industries, became and remains the top producer of center pivot irrigation systems in the world.

GRAND ISLAND TORNADOES

1980

June 3, 1980, was a typical summer day for the folks of Grand Island, Nebraska. The sun was warm and the air slightly humid on that Tuesday. The forecast for Nebraska's third largest city called for a 20 percent chance of thunderstorms.

The youth of Grand Island spent the day at the pool. Adults went to work. At suppertime, families sat down together to eat, discussing the recent eruption of Mount St. Helens and the release of the second movie in the *Star Wars* saga.

A little after 6 p.m., Grand Island residents noticed dark clouds gathering in the sky above their city. In the next two hours, winds picked up and tension in the air seemed to build. Mothers shooed playing children inside and locked the doors tight. Lightning filled the sky. Families grabbed flashlights and battery-powered radios and headed to their basements as the sudden blast of tornado sirens filled the air outside.

The citizens of Grand Island were about to be in the center of the one of the worst storm cells in Nebraska history. That night, in a span of three hours, a total of seven tornadoes would touch down in and around Grand Island, killing five and injuring hundreds. The tornadoes would leave behind nearly three hundred million dollars in damages.

The first tornado touched down at 8:45 p.m. just northwest of Grand Island. This tornado stayed on the ground for nearly an hour, even as the next two tornadoes touched down within the city limits.

The second tornado was a short one, touching down at 9 p.m. and lifting back into the clouds a mere twelve minutes later.

The third tornado of the night was stronger and worked a path of destruction more than three miles long through the middle of Grand Island. It touched down at 9:05 p.m. and lifted at 9:30 p.m. At this time, the first tornado was still working its way through the countryside north of Grand Island.

The fourth tornado was another short one, touching down at 9:46 p.m. and lifting at 9:50 p.m.

The storm raged outside as clocks passed the 10 p.m. hour, but the shrieking winds of the tornadoes seemed to have dissipated. Many residents of Grand Island assumed the worst was over.

They were proven wrong when, at 10:16 p.m., the fifth and deadliest tornado touched down. Hitting residential and business districts alike, the storm left a six-mile trail of destruction before it lifted back into the clouds at 10:28 p.m. Four of the five fatalities occurred during this tornado.

Even before the fifth tornado was done wreaking havoc, the sixth tornado touched down in a more rural area of Grand Island. That was at 10:25 p.m. It lifted ten minutes later.

The final tornado touched down at 10:45 p.m. The storm was moving past the city by now and the mile-wide path of devastation from the seventh tornado was contained to rural areas. The last tornado lifted at 11:30 p.m.

In that three-hour time span, nearly five hundred homes and fifty business were completely destroyed by the multiple tornadoes.

Upon review of satellite images obtained in the weeks following the disaster, meteorologists were able to determine that the super storm cell was extremely slow moving, clocking in at only eight miles per hour. While most tornadoes move in a north-northeasterly direction, this cell moved to the south-southeast. Three of the seven tornadoes were anticyclonic, which meant they moved in a clockwise direction. In the northern hemisphere, more than 99 percent of tornadoes move in a counter-clockwise direction. The tornadoes did also not move in anything resembling a straight line and several looped around and around, retracing their own paths of devastation. Three of the tornadoes were categorized as F1 tornadoes, with wind speeds between 73 and 112 miles per hour. One tornado was an F2, with winds up to 157 miles per hour. Two tornadoes were categorized as F3s, meaning wind speeds were up to 206 miles per hour. The largest tornado of the evening, the fifth one to touch down, was the only one to be named an F4 tornado. Wind speeds during that time were clocked at 251 miles per hour.

All in all that night, tornadoes were on the ground for two hours and twenty minutes total.

When Grand Island citizens emerged from their basements and safe places, they were surrounded by devastation. Buildings and houses looked like piles of sticks. Hundred-year-old trees in the city park were flattened, broken off at the bases of the trunks. Power was out throughout town for days and the city's sewage system was not operational. The veterans' home suffered so much damage that patients had to be moved to facilities in Lincoln and Omaha to be able to receive care.

Police dogs were brought in to search for missing persons and a curfew was put into effect. Police reports show several people were arrested for violating curfew, but looting was kept to a minimum.

City officials had much to deal with following the devastation. One problem they encountered was regarding the disposal of debris. They filled the inner field at the Fonner Park horseracing track with debris, which was then burned and compacted. Another location for dumping debris was in Ryder Park. For about six weeks following the tornado, debris was piled in a circle about two hundred feet in diameter reaching forty feet high. After the pile had been burned and compacted, it was seeded for grass and is now a popular sledding hill during the winter months. The pile is known today as Tornado Hill.

The Grand Island tornadoes made national news because of the unique formation of the storm and its devastation. A children's book, titled *Night of the Twisters,* was based on the events of that evening and was later made into a television movie. President Jimmy Carter came to Nebraska and toured Grand Island a week following the tornadoes.

As time passed, so did the public eye. There have been other tornadoes and natural disasters that have replaced the Grand Island event in the history books. But, to the residents of that community who lived through it, June 3, 1980, will be forever etched in their minds.

SANDHILL CRANES

Every Year

From mid-February to mid-April every year, thousands of lesser sandhill cranes, five hundred thousand to be exact, descend upon an eighty-mile stretch of the Platte River valley between Kearney and Grand Island.

The largest gathering of any species of crane anywhere in the world, the annual migratory rest stop has found a perfect area in the Platte River valley. The shallow water of the Platte twists around sandbars and wetlands, creating safe havens for the cranes. The sandbars are far from predators who prowl the banks to the north and south, and the wetlands provide insects and worms to help feed the cranes.

With long spindly legs stretching out beneath solid grey bodies, 80 percent of the world's population of sandhill cranes make their home in Nebraska for usually about a month during the migratory period. Numbers peak at mid-March as the cranes make their way north from their winter lands in Arizona, New Mexico, Texas, and Mexico. After resting up and eating their fill along the Platte River, the cranes move on to their summer homes across the plains of Canada, into Alaska, and even across the Bering Strait into Siberia.

Thought to be the oldest species of bird alive on the planet today, sandhill cranes travel up to ten thousand miles on their annual migration, flying three hundred to five hundred miles per day in the spring. Their nesting grounds along the Platte River in Nebraska are visualized as the pinch of an hourglass in the whole scheme of the sandhill cranes' territory.

Sandhill cranes are joined by roughly ten million other waterfowl, including ducks, geese, and even the endangered whooping crane, on the fertile plains of Nebraska. Although the birds do feed on the insects and worms found in the river basin, they also branch out to nearby farmlands, feasting on grain and seed, mainly corn, left in the fields.

During their time in Nebraska, the cranes can gain up to 20 percent of their body weight, or nearly two pounds. The cranes use this time as a rest stop halfway along their migratory journey and also as a time to gather fat and energy to make the final push north.

When the cranes start to arrive in the Platte River valley, so do the tourists. Humans flock by the thousands to several protected sites along the river, including the Rowe Sanctuary, first established by the National Audubon Society in 1974. The sanctuary, which started out as 728 acres of protected land, has been joined by other conservation and government agencies over the years. Now, nearly fourteen thousand acres of grasslands and wetlands along the Platte are safe.

Most protected lands offer observation and photography blinds for the birdwatchers who come to visit. Many area farmers have replanted their land with native Nebraska grasses in an effort to increase roosting sites and diverse food options for the cranes.

Arriving in flocks numbering in the hundreds, the cranes swarm together so closely it is nearly impossible to see through the dense cloud of feathers. Lines and lines of cranes land along the Platte River daily from February to April, with each crane or bonded pair of cranes searching for a rest place to call their own for a few weeks. Sandhill cranes can be aggressive when it comes to territory and food; usually a loud trumpet call from an offended bird is enough to settle the matter of ownership.

After a few weeks of rest and gluttony, the cranes begin to make their departure. They rise above the Platte River in a graceful dance, turn their beaks to the north, and move on. They'll be back next spring to feast and rejuvenate on the fertile Nebraska plains.

NEBRASKA FACTS AND TRIVIA

- Nebraska was the thirty-seventh state to join the United States of America.

- The word Nebraska comes from the Oto Indian word for "flat water."

- The state capital of Nebraska is Lincoln.

- Omaha is the largest city.

- Nebraska has a population of around 1.7 million residents.

- Nebraska is 77,358 square miles, and the sixteenth largest state in America.

- There are ninety-three counties in Nebraska.

- The state's highest point is Panorama Point at 5,426 feet above sea level.

- Nebraska's state motto is "Equality Before the Law."

- The state bird is the western meadowlark.

- The state tree is the cottonwood.

- The state mammal is the white-tailed deer.

- The state fish is the channel catfish.

- The state fossil is the woolly mammoth.

- The state insect is the honeybee.

- The state flower is the goldenrod.

- The state grass is little bluestem.

- The state rock is the prairie agate.

- The state gemstone is the blue chalcedony.

- The state soil is holdrege.

- The state beverage is milk.

- The state soft drink is Kool-Aid.

- Nebraska was first known as the Tree Planter's State. Since 1945, the official nickname has been the Cornhusker State.

- Aviator Charles Lindbergh learned to fly at Ray Page's Flying School in Lincoln in 1922.

- Omaha's Henry Doorly Zoo is home to the world's largest indoor rainforest and largest indoor desert.

- The world's largest porch swing is located in Hebron and can seat twenty-four people at one time.

- The National Museum of Roller Skating is located in Lincoln.

- Longtime television host Johnny Carson was raised in Norfolk and had his first television job for WOW in Omaha.

- Nebraska has more miles of river than any other state.

- Alliance is home to Carhenge, a near-exact replica of England's Stonehenge, but made from old cars.

- The largest private collection of all things Americana is housed at Pioneer Village in Minden.

- Nebraska's Susan LaFlesche Picotte, born near Macy in 1865, was the first Native American female to earn a medical degree in the United States.

- Residents of Niobrara, located on the confluence of the Niobrara and Missouri Rivers, have moved the entire town due to flooding not once, but twice, in the town's history. The current location is the third to house the community.

- During World War II, the Naval Ammunition Depot in Hastings supplied 40 percent of all ammunition to American troops, making it the largest ammunition depot in the country.

- Omaha is the birthplace of the Reuben sandwich, a concoction of corned beef, Swiss cheese, and sauerkraut on rye bread.

- Nearly the entire state of Nebraska covers the Ogallala Aquifer, a vast underground water table. The aquifer provides water for drinking and irrigation for most of the Great Plains.

- Nebraska was the first state to complete its portion of the nation's interstate system, a 455-mile stretch of four-lane highway.

- The 911 emergency call system was first developed in Lincoln.

- The NCAA College World Series has been held in Omaha annually since 1950, first in Johnny Rosenblatt Stadium then in TD Ameritrade Park.

- When Major Stephen Long surveyed Nebraska in 1823, he cited the area on his map with the words "Great American Desert," saying nothing would grow on the vast, arid prairie.

- The sand hills of western Nebraska are home to the largest area of grass-covered sand dunes in North America. The only places in the world with more sand are the Sahara and Arabian Deserts.

- Andrew Higgins, a native of Columbus, designed the front-opening landing craft that was instrumental in the Allies' successful storming of the Normandy beaches on D-Day.

- Wahoo, Nebraska, with a 2010 population of 3,984, is the birthplace of a Nobel Prize–winning physiologist, a Pulitzer-winning composer, and a member of Major League Baseball's Hall of Fame. They are, respectively, Dr. George Beadle, Howard Hanson, and "Wahoo Sam" Crawford.

- Clarence S. Irvine, a lieutenant general in the Air Force, set a number of speed and distance records while piloting bombers in the 1940s. One of his achievements was a thirty-nine-hour non-stop flight from Honolulu to Cairo in 1946. He was a native of St. Paul, Nebraska.

- Cherry County has more cows than people. Cherry County is also larger than the state of Connecticut.

- The University of Nebraska–Lincoln football team has been known as the Cornhuskers since 1900. Prior to that date, their nicknames included Old Gold Knights, Antelopes, Rattlesnake Boys, and even Bugeaters.

BIBLIOGRAPHY

Books

Ambrose, Stephen E. *Undaunted Courage.* New York: Touchstone, 1996.

Bartels, Diane Ruth Armour. *Sharpie.* Lincoln, Nebraska: Dageforde Publishing, 1996.

Beret's Nebraska Historical Markers & Sites. Sioux Falls, South Dakota: Brevet Press, 1974.

Birding Nebraska. Lincoln, Nebraska: *NEBRASKAland* magazine, 2004.

Buecker, Thomas R. *Fort Robinson and the American West, 1874–1899.* Norman, Oklahoma: University of Oklahoma Press, 1999.

The Cellars of Time: Paleontology and Archaeology in Nebraska. Lincoln, Nebraska: *NEBRASKAland* magazine, 1994.

Corkery, Paul. *Carson: The Unauthorized Biography.* New York: Randt & Company, 1987.

Creigh, Dorothy Weyer. *Nebraska.* Nashville, Tennessee: American Association for State and Local History, 1977.

Endorf, Charlotte M. *Plains Bound: Fragile Cargo.* Denver, Colorado: Outskirts Press, 2005.

Forsberg, Michael. *On Ancient Wings.* Lincoln, Nebraska: Michael Forsberg Photography, 2004.

Fort Robinson Illustrated. Lincoln, Nebraska: *NEBRASKAland* magazine, 1986.

Hickey, Donald R. *Nebraska Moments.* Lincoln, Nebraska: University of Nebraska Press, 2007.

Historic Places: The National Register for Nebraska. Lincoln, Nebraska: Nebraska Game & Parks Commission, 1989.

Luebke, Frederick C. *Nebraska: An Illustrated History.* Lincoln, Nebraska: University of Nebraska Press, 1995.

Majors, Alexander. *Seventy Years on the Frontier.* Lincoln, Nebraska: University of Nebraska Press, 1989.

Moulton, Gary E. *The Lewis and Clark Journals.* Lincoln, Nebraska: University of Nebraska Press, 2003.

Oberdieck, William. *America's Prisoner of War.* New York: Carlton Press Corp., 1995.

Oldham, Byron W. *The Prairie Motor Venture.* Nebraska City.

Olson, James C. *J. Sterling Morton.* Lincoln, Nebraska: Nebraska State Historical Society Foundation, 1972.

Paul, R. Eli. *The Nebraska Indian Wars Reader 1865–1877.* Lincoln, Nebraska: University of Nebraska Press, 1998.

Ramsey, William E., and Betty Dineen Shrier. *Doorway to Freedom.* Ontario, Canada: Mosaic Press, 2008.

Reisdorff, James J. *North Platte Canteen.* David City, Nebraska: South Platte Press, 1986.

Starita, Joe. *I Am a Man.* New York: St. Martin's Press, 2008.

Voorhies, Dr. Michael R. *Nebraska Wildlife Ten Million Years Ago.* Lincoln, Nebraska: University of Nebraska State Museum.

BIBLIOGRAPHY

Articles

Gardner, Robert. "Constructing a Technological Forest: Nature, Culture, and Tree-Planting in the Nebraska Sand Hills." *Environmental History* 14.2 (2009): 53 pars. 30 Mar. 2010.

Interviews

Crook, Dr. Sara B., Peru State College. Personal interview. November 2010.

Letters

Bessey, Dr. Charles E. Letter to President Theodore Roosevelt. Bessey Ranger District. Halsey, Nebraska. January 25, 1902.

Pamphlets

Ashfall Fossil Beds. Lincoln, Nebraska: Nebraska Game & Parks Commission.

Little Church of Keystone, Nebraska. Little Church of Keystone.

Documentaries

Most Honorable Son. Dir. Bill Kubota. KDN Films, 2007.

Websites

www.visitnebraska.gov. Accessed 2011.

www.stromsburglibrary.com/flippin.htm. Accessed July 6, 2011.

www.nebraskahistory.org. Accessed 2011.

www.johnnycarson.com. Accessed 2011.

www.gitwisters.com. Accessed November 2011.

www.crh.noaa.gov. Accessed November 2011.

INDEX

INDEX

ABOUT THE AUTHOR

Tammy Partsch was born and raised in Nebraska. In addition to writing, she organizes tours at Arbor Day Farm and plays the piano for a local high school choir. Her past experiences include being a photographer, a bookseller, a journalist, a radio broadcaster, and a travel agent. Tammy lives in her hometown of Nebraska City with her high school sweetheart, Dave, and their son, Luke.